Still We Rise

# Still We Rise

*A Love Letter to the Southern Biscuit with Over 70 Sweet and Savory Recipes*

Erika Council

PHOTOGRAPHS BY ANDREW THOMAS LEE

Clarkson Potter/Publishers
New York

For my biggest supporters and cheerleaders on this journey, my daughter Kamaya, son Charlie, and husband Charles

# Contents

## 6. SWEET BISCUITS

## 7. SPREAD LOVE LIKE BUTTER: JAMS, SPREADS, AND BUTTERS TO JAZZ UP YOUR BISCUITS

## 8. BISCUIT BREAKFAST AND BRUNCH

# Introduction

*When I decided to write a cookbook, I had little doubt that it would be* about the gospel of biscuits. They've long been an obsession of mine, one that matured from a family tradition, to a hobby, to a business. As the years have passed, biscuits have taken center stage in my life, such that now, while it's still dark outside, our little biscuit bakery radiates with light and warmth from both the ovens and the people working inside. The golden glow the sun casts over the city as it rises mimics the golden-brown tops of the biscuits coming out of the oven on their trays.

Like many people in the South, I have always had biscuits nearby, but I grew up very aware of the legacy of two women's biscuits in particular.

My paternal grandmother, Mildred Edna Cotton Council, was an icon in the culinary industry, paving the way not only for me but for many others. Born in 1929, she led an extraordinary life, one that she chronicled in her 1999 cookbook, *Mama Dip's Kitchen*, named after her beloved restaurant. The youngest of seven children, my grandma Dip was born and raised on a farm in the Chatham County area of North Carolina. She earned the nickname "Dip" due to her height; she stood a regal six feet and could reach down into the rain barrels to collect water for the kitchen when the wells ran dry. She had eight children, one being my father, William Council (who thinks he makes the best pimento cheese). And in 1976, she opened her restaurant in the college town of Chapel Hill, North Carolina, with just enough money to buy food for the breakfast service that day. As they say, the rest is history—a legacy that thrives today over forty years later, upheld by Aunts Spring, Annette "Niecy," Sandra, and Cousins Tonya and Cissy, who are truly the keepers of the flame.

But growing up, when I would spend time in the family business, I would watch them make and fill basket after basket of biscuits.

My maternal grandmother wasn't as famous for her cooking, but Geraldine Dortch was an educator who carried her then-rare advanced degree from Columbia University back home with her to the small town of Goldsboro, North Carolina, and became known as Granny to just about everyone in the community.

She once told me a story from early on in her time up North: my grandmother and a fellow student were in a restaurant and ordered a meal that came with a basket of what she called biscuit rolls. She said there was a white couple who sat next to them and they got to chatting, asking each other questions, and even eating together. Being from the Jim Crow South, she was amazed that they could simply eat and talk together, and I think of that story of togetherness when I make biscuits now, too.

I've just always loved making biscuits and making my biscuits the bomb. As for how I went from making bomb biscuits to making the Bomb Biscuit Company, I'd been working for years as a software engineer in Atlanta, but in 2016, I started baking biscuits as a pop-up, and my dear friends Bryan, Matt, and Jesse allowed me to host a pop-up Sunday supper at their restaurant, Kimball House.

It was here that I met Bryan Furman. I'd eaten at Bryan's BBQ spot before, one of the only places I knew in Atlanta that had food that tasted like what I grew up with. While his signature peach mustard sauce celebrates his South Carolina roots, his chopped pork sandwich is the only one I've found to bring me as much joy as eastern Carolina BBQ. Also, Bryan's hash and rice is unmatched. Quote me on that. So, when we first met, I told him such, and he sang praises about my biscuits and apple butter, inviting me to stop by his new restaurant. We caught up a few weeks later, me bearing a quart container of apple butter and a bag of biscuits. I stood outside near his smoker, and we talked about everything from African American–owned hog farms to retro Air Jordans. Bryan told me about a talented chef, Mike Sheats, and his equally talented wife, Shyretha, and their idea to collaborate on a Black History Month dinner. One late afternoon, we formed a plan that resulted in a sold-out dinner celebrating the art and greatness of the Black cooks and chefs that came before, made by those paving the way forward in the present.

"I'm here smoking meats anyway, so why not?" was Bryan's response when I brought up the idea of a breakfast pop-up at his restaurant. It was exactly like him: no-nonsense and full of generosity. So, one Saturday morning, we opened with fried chicken biscuits, cinnamon rolls, and the like. To say we were unprepared would be an understatement. We ran out of biscuits within the first hour, and I ran to make more. A few friends pitched in to expedite orders and help manage a line that wrapped around the building. It was both exhausting and exhilarating. Afterward, Bryan turned to me, laughing, and said, "Hell yeah, E, what I tell you!"

Bomb Biscuit Co. came to life after Bryan's kind offer to host that pop-up, and it ran for a couple of years out of the back kitchen next

## BISCUIT LOVE

You know that feeling when a relationship is new? You yearn to be close to them, to breathe them in, to fuse together until you're the same person filling the same space. I had that once with a man who checked all the boxes.

Let's call him HB—for Hershey Bar. One morning after HB and I had dated for a few months, I got up early to make biscuits. They rose high with glossy, crisp tops, due to the buttermilk I'd brushed them with before baking. My kitchen smelled like my granny's house, and heaven. In other words: *Your girl DID THAT!*

HB strolled into the kitchen and praised the wonderful smell. He took a long look at the spread I'd prepared, then looked at me with a smile and said, "I normally just skip breakfast."

*Oh OK, that's fine . . . I guess?!*

As he chugged a glass of orange juice, I consoled myself with the thought that no one is perfect. And who was I to judge a person on his life choices, no matter how . . . umm . . . abhorrent? Soon HB sidled up to me and put

*Still We Rise*

an arm around my waist. As he inhaled into my neck, my earlier judgments about his breakfast blunder started to fade away, and I began to simmer with a feeling that I should probably not go into detail about in a cookbook.

Then he asked, "Are these dinner rolls?"

"What?" The fog started to clear.

"Dinner rolls for breakfast; that seems like a lot," he said.

"No, those are biscuits," I stammered in disbelief.

"Dinner rolls, biscuits, buns. They're all the same, aren't they? I'm not a fan of any of them really," he murmured.

I haven't seen that dude in decades, but my beloved buttermilk biscuits have always been with me in times of triumph and trouble.

to Bryan's pits. It took further shape as we served at farmers' markets and catered for corporate clients and weddings. My anti-opening-a-restaurant attitude wavered a little, and my husband and I started looking at commercial properties. Then the pandemic hit and put us and the world in time-out, confining us to our homes, like when Granny used to make us kids sit in the corner for acting up at church.

Like many other small business owners, I found myself trying to figure out how to pivot, or shutter. Then I got a call from the owner of a company that I had catered breakfast for, asking if it was possible to have orders sent to his staff, who were working from home. My daughter, home from college, rode along with me as I went to twenty different addresses dropping off fresh biscuits. People would come out and say hi, striking up a conversation from their front porch.

Later I wrote to other people I'd catered for, and 2020 saw us hitting up hundreds of doorsteps, dropping off biscuits, jam, cinnamon rolls, and pies. Eventually we pitched a tent in the middle of the Summerhill neighborhood offering pickups, and finally in 2021, we opened the doors at our restaurant, Bomb Biscuit Co. Our menu includes a multitude of biscuit sandwiches, from our most popular, lemon pepper fried chicken, to old-school classics like fried green tomatoes. Our customers have become like family, with people coming all the way from New Zealand for a hot fried chicken biscuit.

The bakery is in the Old Fourth Ward area, a historic district of Atlanta, best known as the birthplace of Martin Luther King Jr. and home of the Ebenezer Baptist Church. Heading into work each day, turning into the neighborhood, I drive down Auburn Avenue, which once was flourishing economically with scores of African American businesses, churches, newspaper publishers, and nightclubs. Due to the tidal wave of gentrification, the neighborhood looks much different now with African American–owned businesses no longer as prominent as they once were. So I take pride in the fact that I've found a place here, and for however long that may be, we're doing our best to embody the spirit of Black entrepreneurship and setting a table for everyone, like Mama Dip did—and like Granny taught me about.

Although much has been written about biscuits, I felt something was always missing from those stories, something that seemed representative of me. In my research into biscuit books, none highlighted the contributions of Black bakers and chefs, yet my entire education on this subject has been guided by Black hands. Some by direct instruction, others by osmosis. This cookbook is a love letter to the African American women and men who have both inspired and taught me along the way. As my mother would say, "They're still here, because I'm still here." By the end of this cookbook, you'll know them all a little bit, and a little more about me, plus everything you need to know to be a bomb biscuit baker.

# Hidden . . . or Erased?

Several years back, I was invited to participate in a dinner soiree hosted by an acclaimed chef and restaurateur here in Atlanta. The event was part of a series, put on in partnership with an association that was once described to me as the "Culinary Oscars." So, to be recognized on this scale caught me off guard in a good way. I was elated. At that time, it was just me running a small pop-up dinner series a few times a month. I'd yet to open a restaurant; I wasn't even working in one. A slightly nervous wreck, I gave myself a pep talk and got on with figuring out what to make.

The event was a multicourse meal made by a talented roster of chefs, all female, with me being one of only two women of color in the lineup (unfortunately a recurring theme). Since I'd picked the dessert course, I was one of the last to present. My apprehension about my dish was for nothing because everything went wonderfully . . . until the photographer made his way to my table. We were plating sweet potato cakes with benne seed brittle on beautiful white china with gold trim. The dish was an homage to both my great-aunt Mabel, who crunched and munched on this brittle for decades, and my love of the sweet potato pie that has graced numerous Sunday dinner tables.

As the photographer walked around taking photos, he kept asking the white chefs standing nearby to act as though they were sprinkling the brittle over the plates. A few complied, but one told the gentleman he should get shots of me since it was my dish. He took a single photo as I was turning away. With a shrug, I walked out the door and told the diners about my sweet potato cake and the Black women it paid homage to, calling off a litany of names of iconic chefs and writers, most of whom the audience had never heard of. When the images were released, there were beautiful shots of all the dishes presented that evening, including mine—with white hands sprinkling brittle over the sweet potato cake.

Once, I shared an article with my mother that talked about culinary "hidden figures." She bristled at the title, asking, "Were they hidden or erased?" I remembered this conversation and the way I felt seeing myself removed from something I'd labored over. So I guess you could say it was both. This feeling returned one evening, after enjoying one of the best meals I'd ever had with some friends. The boisterous restaurant owner came out to greet us, hearing there were people in town as part of a foodways conference, and struck up a conversation. He was the embodiment of entitlement, which soured the evening. Eventually, he turned to me, the only person of color in the group, and told me to come with him so he could introduce me to "the Black woman in the back that cooks most of the food." The entire table went silent, as I imagined this interaction being the first such they had ever borne witness to. For a moment, I contemplated walking out, but instead I stood and made my way to the back where the kitchen was located. Standing in her white chef's coat and slacks, a luminous woman with silver-streaked hair looked up and smiled warmly at me while we both ignored the ignorant owner hovering over to the side. I thanked her for the wonderful meal she put together for us, and we talked for a few minutes before she squeezed my hand and told me to take care and keep cooking.

Black women are so often erased from the contributions we make. No matter how many times it happens, the sting never dulls.

# 1.
# BISCUIT
# BEGINNINGS

*Behind the Pantry Door*

# Ingredients

*My great-aunt Mabel—I'll make a few references to her in this book—* lived in the house that was built by my great-grandfather, affectionately known as Big Daddy. It was a very large, older house that I'm sure was (or is) haunted, with a large pantry off the kitchen. As kids, when we were in trouble, we were sent there to sit and think about how our actions have consequences. This was supposed to be punishment, but I loved it, pretending I was some queen locked away in a tower, held hostage by jars of legumes and bags of cornstarch. I'd take the time to read the labels on food products and count how many different colored beans were in the jars until my eyes crossed. Once, when my granny came to let me out of my pantry prison, she asked if I'd learned anything. I answered by telling her that I found four cans of expired milk behind the peanut butter.

You'll need quite a few items out of the pantry and fridge to bake and cook your way through this book, and none of them are expired milk. Here are the basics.

## FLOUR

My introduction to flour came in the form of a warning to be sure to moisturize so I did not go to school looking like I'd been crawling through it. In other words, don't be ashy. Luckily, the hundred pounds of Vaseline and blue Bergamot grease my mother doused me in as a kid allowed me to achieve this to some degree of success. Yet, I've ultimately failed as an adult. Because while I don't crawl through flour, at least not on good days, I spend a great deal of time rolling in it.

Flour can be made from grinding a variety of raw grains, nuts, seeds, roots, and beans. It is also what you will need to bake everything in this book, so let us dive a little deeper into the different variations of the main character of this cookbook. Wheat flour is categorized by its protein content, and higher-protein flours, mostly made from hard wheat, are used to develop gluten for breads. By contrast, low-protein flours are used to make tender, flaky biscuits, cakes, and pie crusts.

All-Purpose Flour: As the name suggests, this is a versatile, general-use wheat flour, milled from hard red wheat or a blend of hard and soft wheats, depending on the brand. All-purpose flour is available commercially as bleached and unbleached, which tells you how the flour was aged. Technically, all flour is bleached, but the process varies. Bleached flour is treated with chemicals such as chlorine dioxide and benzoyl peroxide to speed up the aging process. This results in a whiter, finer-grain flour that produces quick breads, muffins, and pancakes with a softer texture. However, when you're looking to make a biscuit sturdy enough to hold layers of fried chicken, or crispy bacon, eggs, and cheese piled high, without crumbling as soon as you bite into it, my preference is to use unbleached flour.

Unbleached flour is aged naturally, with a more off-white tint and dense grain. The denser grain adds more structure to baked goods like yeast breads.

At Bomb Biscuit Co. we use King Arthur brand flour, and all the recipes in this book were made with it unless otherwise specified. But let's be clear, for most of history, there was no brand-specific flour

when it came to making biscuits. They were made with whatever was on hand.

A few recipes call for other types of flour, so let's break those down.

Self-Rising Flour: Hands down the most popular flour of choice when it comes to biscuit making in the South, with White Lily brand being the most referenced. Self-rising flour is just that: it will rise by itself due to the baking powder and salt already added. White Lily self-rising flour is the leading actress in a lot of the biscuit recipes I've seen. While I agree she makes the flakiest biscuits, White Lily can be hard to find if you live outside the South, so I'll also provide a quick method for making your own self-rising flour if you're unable to find it.

Whole Wheat Flour: It's not what you would automatically think to grab when making biscuits. The bran and germ of the wheat grain make this flour more nutrient rich and give it a slightly darker color. Also because the bran absorbs more water, any recipe using whole wheat flour requires an increase in liquid volume as well. Whole wheat flour has a shorter shelf life, so I recommend storing it in the fridge or freezer.

Gluten-Free Flour: Hats off to every baker, chef, home cook, and alien life force that has perfected the art of gluten-free baking. It is not to be trifled with. Xanthan gum, arrowroot starch, potato flour, and thoughts and prayers have become staple items we keep on hand for our gluten-free biscuits. I use Cup4Cup Gluten Free Multipurpose Flour, which works the best with the recipes I've developed. There are a lot of gluten-free mixes and flours on the market, and I'm fairly sure I have tried them all, with varying degrees of success.

Graham Flour: When I started on this biscuit cookbook journey, I wanted to make sure that most of the ingredients were easily accessible. While it is possible that butter churned by golden fairies who live off the coast of France might make the best biscuits, I also think it is important to note that Big Mama and all the church ladies with the blue-ribbon recipes used what they had and produced some of the best baked goods you'll ever find. That being said, I've got a kick-ass biscuit recipe that calls for graham flour that we get from Anson Mills. So there is a bit of fancy in this book that will absolutely have my mother throwing me the biggest side-eye when she reads this.

**Cornmeal:** Of course! While people might say that biscuits are my thing, cornbread is inarguably my absolute favorite quick bread. Cornmeal is dried and ground field corn. In this book, the recipes call for fine- to medium-ground cornmeal. Not self-rising or Jiffy—please put that back. As a side note: My great-aunt Mabel made the best cornbread in the world. I said if I ever wrote a cookbook, I'd fit that note in somewhere. May she rest in eternal peace knowing that I now add a ridiculous amount of sugar to my cornbread in her honor.

## FATS

Fats come in both liquid and solid forms and add richness and moisture to biscuits. They work to coat the proteins in flour, creating a boundary between the water and the proteins. This shortens and weakens the gluten strands, creating delicate cakes and tender breads. Throughout this book, you will use several types of fat to achieve biscuit greatness.

**Butter:** Fat made by churning the cream from cows' milk. Used generously throughout this book, butter is inherently tasty. We'll use both unsalted and salted butter.

**Vegetable Shortening:** One important feature of a southern kitchen, at least the ones I have had the pleasure of dining in, is the blue jar of Crisco that sits on the counter or above the stove. My aunt would tell you that is how you can gauge whether someone could cook. There was never actual shortening in that jar, just congealed bacon drippings that got redistributed liberally in about everything from green beans to cornbread, but we will get to the

gospel of bacon fat later. Let us talk about shortening. Crisco, specifically, is a mash-up of palm, soy, and canola oils. In most older cookbooks, the fat used for biscuit making was lard, but with the commercial introduction of Crisco, which was much cheaper, the lard was replaced with shortening. Unlike lard, which can carry the flavor of the hog into your baked goods, shortening has a neutral taste—and a much longer shelf life than butter. It also has a high smoke point for frying. So much versatility in one blue jar, it truly is King Crisco. We'll use shortening in several biscuits throughout the book as well.

**Bacon Grease:** After removing those sizzling bacon strips from the stove, you must drain the leftover grease into a jar for later use because it is a sin to be wasteful, and those turnip greens need a touch of bacon fat to taste right according to the handbook of great cooks. Bacon fat was also used in pies and biscuits. I'll say, bacon fat (and lard) is my favorite fat to use to make biscuits. Perhaps this is because it was the fat of choice in the biscuits of my childhood, and the nostalgia has a tight grip on my flavor profile. Or as my mother said once, we are from North Carolina, so we're inclined to have a fondness for pork.

**Lard:** Historically, biscuits were more commonly made with lard than butter. Lard can come in rendered and unrendered forms. Unrendered lard is just trimmed pig fat. I would not recommend this for baking, but if you ask a dear friend who is one of the best pitmasters around for a few pints of lard, this is what he might hand you. True story. So let us be precise with our request going forward. Rendered lard is what you use in baking. It's still pork fat, but it's been melted and filtered, then chilled. This helps remove some of the lingering pork flavor that you may not want to permeate your pie crust. Lard comes from the fatty parts of the pig, like the belly, shoulder, and butt. The superior version is leaf lard. It is derived from the leaf-shaped fat around the kidneys and abdomen. Its texture is ultrasmooth, and it produces the creamiest biscuits you have ever tasted. If you, like one of my closest friends, are anti-meat anything—especially pork—I realize this all sounds gross to you, and I apologize. There are lots of biscuits in this book just for y'all, so don't close the book just yet!

**Duck Fat:** This creates a flaky and tender texture in baked goods. In the recipe for Duck Fat Biscuits on page 59, it's used in place of lard.

**Peanut Butter:** The peanuts that are roasted and then ground to create the peanut butter spread we buy in the store are full of fat and can be used in baked goods, like the Peanut Butter and Cane Syrup Biscuits on page 137.

## LIQUIDS

Liquids add moisture, flavor, and in some instances, acidity to activate the leavening agents in your dry mix. Not adding enough liquid leads to dry and crumbly biscuits, and, friends, we're not going to have any of that. Let's take a look at the different types of liquids you'll use throughout this book.

**Buttermilk:** Traditionally, this is the liquid byproduct left over from churning butter. Prior to the emergence of homogenization, the milk was left out to permit the cream and milk to separate, allowing bacteria to form and naturally fermenting the milk. Unlike this byproduct of yesteryear, the buttermilk we purchase now is cultured, made by reintroducing lactic-acid bacteria to pasteurized skim or low-fat milk. The consistency will vary depending on the brand. All this is to say, if you have a recipe that calls for 1 cup of buttermilk, there is a chance that when that recipe was developed, the buttermilk they used could've been thicker or thinner than what you have in your fridge, causing you to add too much or too little liquid. Both lead to mild frustration and annoyance, and I don't want y'all to be in the kitchen mad at me. So, for the recipes in this book that call for it, use full-fat buttermilk. If you can only find low-fat buttermilk, decrease the amount called for by ¼ cup and add back a tablespoon at a time as needed.

**Whole Milk:** This is sometimes referred to as regular milk and contains around 3.25 percent milk fat. The creaminess, fat, sugar, and protein content make it an ideal liquid for whipping up delectable baked goods. Whole milk also supports browning and keeps the texture of your baked goods light. Therefore, I will sometimes brush a little whole milk on the biscuits before putting them in the oven. Many years ago, while living in a small town in South Carolina, I met a woman who made biscuits using whole milk with a tablespoon or two of cornstarch whisked in a bowl. She proceeded to mash cooked rice into the milk slurry before mixing it into the dry ingredients. The technique and the biscuits blew me away. When I asked where she learned it, she let me know that her family never used buttermilk for biscuits. Whole or canned milk was all they had. And rice, plenty of rice. So that is what they used. Many of the biscuit recipes that I've found in older African American–authored cookbooks list "milk" or "a can of milk" as the liquid needed.

**Evaporated Canned Milk:** A shelf-stable product that's made by removing water from fresh milk and then heating it, which gives it a slightly cooked taste and darker color. It's also the secret ingredient in many church ladies' mac and cheese recipes.

**Yogurt and Kefir:** Both are made with cows' milk, much like buttermilk. However, yogurt is made with cultured bacteria, while kefir—"drinkable yogurt" as my husband calls it—is made with kefir grain. We will use both in this book in place of buttermilk.

**Heavy Cream:** This has one of the highest fat contents among dairy products. Also called heavy whipping cream, it is the thickest part of the milk that rises to the top. All that fat keeps heavy cream in constant rotation in biscuit recipes.

**Sour Cream:** Another fermented dairy product that adds moisture to baked goods. Sour cream also has a high fat content and plenty of acidity to activate baking soda and help those biscuits rise to great heights.

*Still We Rise*

Leavening agents are essential in the art of baking. They produce gases that form little air bubbles in your dough or batter, causing it to inflate, which gives your baked goods a tall rise and a light texture. In this book we'll use these agents (separately, not all together!) to achieve great biscuits.

**Baking soda** ($NaHCO_3$), or sodium bicarbonate, is a dry powder that reacts to acid, causing carbon dioxide gas to form, which produces little bubbles, which produces the rise we want to see in biscuits. The acids most often used in biscuit baking include buttermilk, yogurt, and sour cream. It is widely written that if you don't have buttermilk, vinegar or lemon juice may be added to whole milk to "form" buttermilk. This works but will *not* get you buttermilk flavor. Please know this and believe me when I tell you my grandma is frowning at y'all adding vinegar to your milk and calling it buttermilk. Still, the acid you have added *will* make those soda biscuits rise like nobody's business, so I will not judge you, at least not today. (However, we will revisit this topic in the recipe for Whole Milk Biscuits on page 53, and I'll judge y'all there.)

**Baking powder** is a mixture of baking soda, a dry acid (traditionally, cream of tartar), and cornstarch. It contains both baking soda and the acid needed to create the carbon dioxide reaction, but they don't react while dry.

Baking powder is often called "double-acting" because the magic happens in two acts. First, leavening occurs when the baking powder gets wet and the baking soda and acid react to each other. When this is dissolved in water and heated, more $CO_2$, or carbon dioxide gas, is released.

This is why most recipes (including the ones in this book) will tell you to mix the dry ingredients together before adding the liquid. It keeps the chemical leaveners from reacting until just before you heat them to preserve that lifting action. It's also why I'll instruct you to mix just until the ingredients are moistened, to minimize the escape of carbon dioxide gas from your batter.

**Yeast,** active dry yeast to be exact, is a dried, granulated form of baker's yeast. Yeast is a biological—rather than chemical—leavener. It's alive, it eats the sugar in your dough, and it releases carbon dioxide gas, which your dough or batter will trap as it rises.

**Steam** is created when a liquid in a recipe heats up in the oven and it tries to escape, lifting the dough. This steam could also come from the water that is naturally inside butter; as the butterfat melts into the dough, the water turns to steam and pushes up on the dough.

## SUGARS

A little sweetness makes everything better, but sugars play multiple roles when it comes to biscuits. In addition to adding flavor, sugars increase browning and tenderize the crumb. Also, sugar acts as the food for yeasted biscuits, like the Angel Biscuits on page 43, increasing rising times. Here is a dive into the sweet side of the ingredients used in this book.

**Granulated Sugar:** Also called white sugar, granulated sugar is most used in baking. Refined from sugar beets or cane, the fine crystals dissolve easily in your baked goods. However, to achieve that bright white color, granulated sugar made from sugar cane requires bone char, making this sugar unsuitable for vegan baked goods.

**Brown Sugar:** Available in light and dark forms. Another refined sugar, brown sugar gets its distinctive brown color and caramel flavor from the addition of molasses. The difference between light and dark brown sugar is simply the amount of molasses it contains.

**Cane Syrup:** One of the South's most treasured sweeteners. It is made by extracting the "juice" from the sugarcane plant and boiling it down to a golden-brown syrup. It's a bit sweeter than molasses and without the bitterness.

**Maple Syrup:** The golden syrup we drench our pancakes in. With hints of caramel, vanilla, and prune, it's much lighter in color and sweeter than cane syrup. It's sometimes used as a substitute for sugar in recipes.

**Honey:** This is my liquid sweetener of choice for biscuits. Made from the nectar of flowering plants, honey is a golden liquid produced by bees. Since it is a humectant, honey retains moisture, which makes it great for biscuits.

## SALT

**Kosher Salt:** The recipes in this book use kosher salt, specifically Diamond Crystal. Shine bright like a diamond and put that iodized salt back in the cabinet. If you only have Morton (the other popular brand), reduce the amount of salt in the recipe by one-third. If you only have regular table salt, reduce the amount by half.

# Tools

*When my husband and I first started dating, I remember visiting his* apartment, thinking how empty the kitchen counters were. Mind you, other than a blender and a toaster, there wasn't really anything else to go on his counter, but even those items were stored in the cabinets. He told me how he really didn't like to have a lot of "stuff" out on the counters. My mom was sure this was a sign of a serial killer, but my granny reassured me it was just that he's from "Up North." Luckily it was neither; he's just very neat. I think about that all these years later as our countertops are full of absolute chaos, albeit neatly organized chaos, but chaos nonetheless. From the convection toaster oven to a small toaster for Pop-Tarts, knife racks, two stand mixers, a Keurig, and lunch boxes, the list is endless. Yes, we have cabinets, but those are full. He truly has the patience of a saint. One evening, I mentioned to him how I was trying to keep the number of tools and equipment needed for this cookbook to a minimum. He laughed hysterically for a good fifteen minutes.

So, here's a list of the tools you'll need to cook your way through this book.

**Mixing Bowls:** Pyrex, stainless steel, plastic. All will work. A range of small, medium, and large mixing bowls should be in every biscuit baker's kitchen.

**Measuring Cups/Spoons:** Used to measure the amount of solid substance or liquid volume.

**Biscuit Cutter:** The size of the biscuits in this book varies from 2 inches to 3½ inches for sandwich-sized biscuits. Each recipe yield is based on the biscuit cutter size. Of course, if you use a larger or smaller size than what is stated in the recipe, you will get a different number of biscuits.

**Bench Scraper:** Sometimes called a bench knife, this tool, which is the size of an index-card (ish), is used to portion hunks of dough as well as to scrape the remnants of dough off countertops and prep tables. We will also use a bench scraper to assist with folding the dough.

**Box Grater:** For butter preparation, some recipes will call for using the slicing side of a box grater. This is the side with the three narrow slits, which is often used for slicing raw vegetables. It produces thin sheets of butter rather than finely shredded pieces. The sheets are then broken into smaller pieces to incorporate into the mixture but will still be large enough to see small visible chunks of butter. Once the biscuits go into the oven, these bits of butter start to melt, creating flaky layers.

**Whisk:** This kitchen tool has a narrow handle and wire loops concatenated together on the opposite end to help blend ingredients thoroughly. All the recipes in this book call for the use of a whisk to mix the dry ingredients.

**Rolling Pin:** Most of the recipes follow the fold and repeat method. This can be accomplished by using your hands, but a rolling pin can be used as well.

**Baking Sheets:** Baking sheet pans to bake off your biscuits are a must. Half sheet pans (18 × 13 inches) work great for home ovens.

**Parchment Paper:** Sometimes butter or cheese in biscuits likes to ooze out along the sides. Parchment paper helps to keep the biscuits from sticking.

**Cast-Iron Skillet:** A well-seasoned skillet is essential for baking several types of biscuits. An 8- or 9-inch skillet will work for the recipes that call for one.

**Food Processor:** You'll need to get a good blend for some of these recipes, like the Strawberry Butter on page 156 you're going to love. A food processor helps to bring all those ingredients together in a flash.

# Techniques

There are two distinct styles of biscuits: rolled or drop, which means they will either be rolled out and cut, or scooped and dropped before baking.

## BEATS BY BISCUITS

Beaten biscuits are the earliest style of biscuits, made without any baking powder or other leaveners, mostly because they weren't readily available. These biscuits were made by repeatedly folding and beating the dough to incorporate air and develop gluten structure, then beating it so long that the gluten strands would eventually break, tenderizing the biscuits. Using a rolling pin or axe handle, this process took over an hour and was often done outdoors, many times by the hands of enslaved cooks. In *What Mrs. Fisher Knows About Old Southern Cooking*, author Abby Fisher instructs the reader to "put the dough on pastry board and beat until perfectly moist and light." After baking, these biscuits had a crisp cracker- or wafer-like exterior with a tender inside. Listen, I've made these biscuits a few times to connect with my biscuit forebears and can say with absolute certainty that taking a rolling pin and beating dough is a fascinating biscuit-making method. However, there won't be any beating of biscuits in this book, mainly because: Who has time for that? Also, I find crying in the walk-in a better stress reliever then beating dough when having a breakdown in the middle of your restaurant.

## LET'S ROLL ON

Most of the recipes in this book use the traditional method of rolling out the biscuit dough and cutting out the rounds with a cutter before baking. Laminating is a folding technique that creates flaky layers when the water in the butter and in the dough converts to steam, puffing up the dough before the steam evaporates. Fold, roll, and repeat. How many times should you roll that biscuit dough? Once, twice? I tend to stop at the third roll, because if you keep rolling, you'll have biscuits the texture of car tires rather than fluffy biscuits—and no one wants that.

## JUST DROP IT

Drop biscuits have more liquid (milk, water, even oil) added to the dough than roll-and-cut biscuits. The dough is much softer—too soft to roll out—which is OK because they're dropped onto the pan or in bubbling hot grease using a large spoon or scoop. Coarser in appearance and texture but just as delicious, drop biscuits tend to be less time consuming as you are skipping the roll-and-cut process and getting straight to the oven after a gentle stir to mix the ingredients. This dough is also great for additions like herbs and cheddar. However, drop biscuits can be a bit crumblier and, in my opinion, don't make the best base for a sandwich.

## CUT IT OUT

Now we've come to the much debated square or circle conversation. To me, this is all a matter of preference. I tend to err on the side of keeping the squares out of my circle, in both life and biscuits, but I can see the value and beauty of a square biscuit. So, I've added a few in this book. Let's talk about the idea that cutting the biscuits in squares eliminates scraps. Not necessarily. Once you reach that final pat or roll in the biscuit-making process, you'll have dough that is sealed around the edges. Square biscuits still require a sharp cut around all sides of the dough; otherwise, the biscuits will really only rise with layers around the sides of the dough that felt the sharp edge of the blade, giving you bookbinder's edges on some of your biscuits. Please no. To truly eliminate biscuit scraps, I learned to roll the dough scraps into a snakelike shape and bake that along with the cut biscuits. You can also make what I call sheet-pan biscuits (Pull-Apart Biscuits, page 76).

For my traditional circle-cut biscuit evangelist, let's talk about the glass cup situation. Actually, let's just put the glass away. Using a drinking glass to cut out your biscuits often presses down and seals the edges of the dough, which will leave you with some very flat biscuits. Use a knife if you don't have biscuit or cookie cutters. Biscuit cutters vary in shape and size. A tin can will work if the edges are sharp enough. Now let's get to it.

*Still We Rise*

# The Basics of Making Biscuits

*Before you grab that mixing bowl and start measuring out flour, let's* break down some biscuit facts and steps. Some of these are found in the good book of *What Big Mama Taught Us*. (This book doesn't really exist, but someone should write it.) And some of them come from my interest in software. Yes, really. Having grown up with a front-row seat to the hardships of the restaurant industry, I quickly decided that would not be the route I took—even though the road led me back there eventually. Instead, I plunged into the world of information technology and stayed there for many years. Designing applications and programs that keep your databases running has carried over into a need to examine and question the processes for just about everything.

While there are tons of recipes for different styles of biscuits in this book, I'm going to walk you through all the steps of the recipe for my homegirl Mrs. Buttermilk and offer you all the pointers, explanations, and tips I would if we were baking a batch of these together in my kitchen.

# The Bomb Buttermilk Biscuit

YIELD: 6 TO 8 BISCUITS

2½ cups / 300 grams
 all-purpose flour, plus extra
 for folding and cutting
1 tablespoon baking powder
1½ teaspoons kosher salt
½ teaspoon baking soda
2 tablespoons / 27 grams
 vegetable shortening, cold,
 cut into ½-inch chunks
1 stick (8 tablespoons) unsalted
 butter, cold
1½ cups full-fat buttermilk, cold

1. Adjust the oven rack to the middle position and preheat the oven to 450°F. This rack position is ideal for baking since it situates the biscuits in the middle of the oven, allowing the hot air to circulate around the pan, resulting in even baking.

2. Place the flour, baking powder, salt, and baking soda in a large bowl and whisk to combine. Whisking the dry ingredients ensures they're evenly distributed. No one wants to bite into a warm biscuit only to find a bitter pocket of baking soda. Whisking also helps to bring air into the flour, making it fluffier and easier to mix with the wet ingredients.

3. Using your fingers, a pastry cutter, or a fork, work the shortening into the flour mixture until only pea-sized pieces remain. Using the slicing side of a box grater, slice the butter into the flour mixture. Toss the sheets of butter in the flour and then lightly work the butter pieces between your fingers or use a pastry cutter to break them up and coat them with flour. Stop when the dough resembles coarse sand and there are still some small visible pieces of butter. Once these pieces of butter melt in the oven, steam will be released and will lift the biscuit, forming tender, flaky layers.

4. Place the biscuit mixture into the freezer for 15 minutes. This helps ensure the butter doesn't soften too much and that it melts only in the oven to create the layer effect.

5. Add the buttermilk to the chilled flour mixture and stir with a spatula until the dough forms into a ball and no dry bits of flour are visible. The dough will be shaggy and sticky.

6. To avoid adding too much liquid to your biscuit mix, start with half of what the recipe calls for and gradually add in the remaining amount until the dough is almost the consistency of Silly Putty.

7. If you do add too much liquid to the dry ingredients, don't just "add more flour" as some recipes call for because your biscuits will not rise as they should, since you've added more flour but not additional leavening ingredients (baking powder and baking soda). Instead of trying to roll them out the traditional way, grab an ice cream scoop or spoon and make them into drop biscuits (page 68).

*Recipe continues*

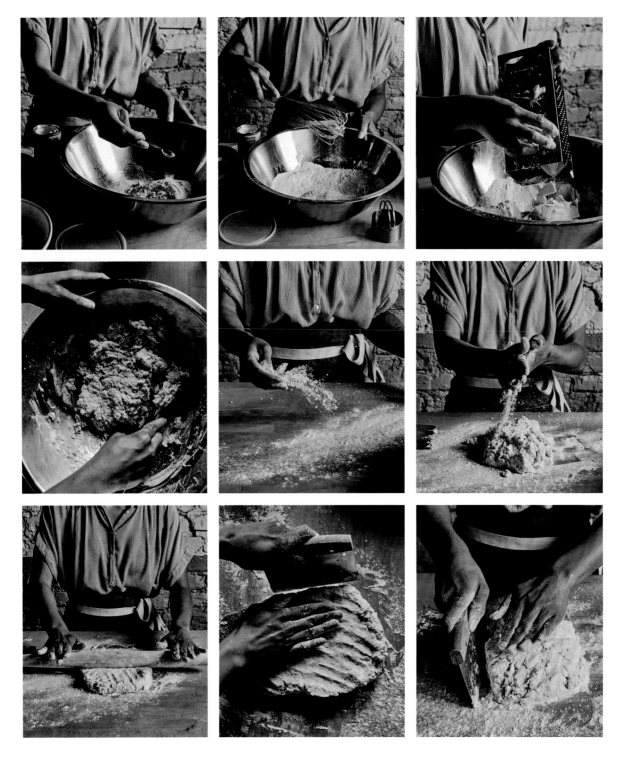

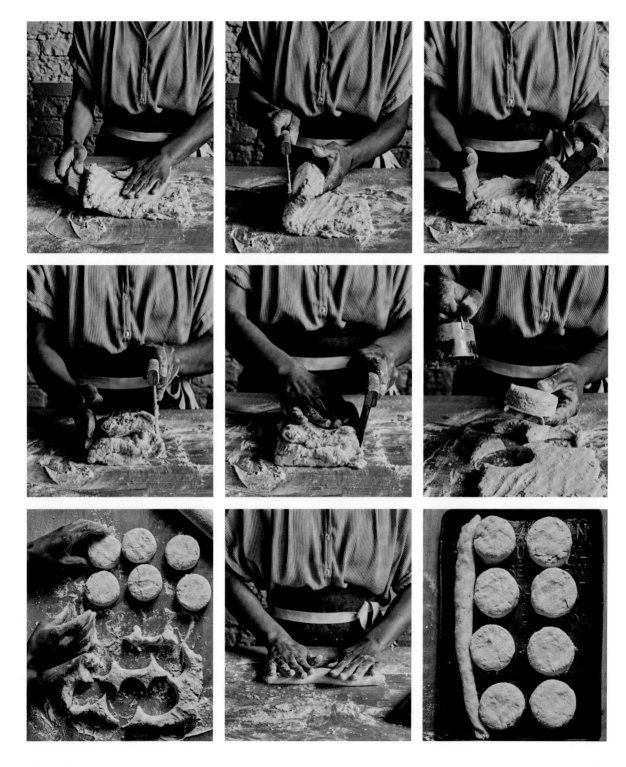

8. Before turning your biscuit dough out onto your work surface, sprinkle the surface with 2 to 3 tablespoons of bench flour. ("Bench flour" is a baker's term for the flour you sprinkle to keep your dough from sticking to the surface as you work with it.) Then lightly dust the top of the dough with flour. Flouring your hands before working the dough also helps to keep it from sticking to you. I like to keep an additional ½ cup of flour off to the side in case I'm in need of some more bench flour. This also keeps the bag or container you store your flour in free from the debris that comes from double-dipping your dough-covered hands into your flour.

9. With floured hands, pat the dough into a ¼-inch-thick rectangle. Fold the ends of the rectangle toward the center, one end on top of the other, to create a trifold. Lightly dust the top of the dough with flour and repeat the process of patting the dough into an 11 × 6 inch ¼-inch-thick rectangle and fold in thirds again. Repeat this step for a third time. Then, pat the dough to a ½-inch thickness. (You can also use a rolling pin for this process.)

10. Cut out the biscuits using a 3½-inch biscuit cutter dipped in flour. It's helpful to dip the cutter in flour before pressing it into the dough to keep the cutter from sticking. Flouring the cutter also helps prevent you from sealing the edges of the cut, which will hinder the biscuits' rise. Be careful to press straight down and do not twist the cutter.

11. Place the biscuit rounds 1 inch apart on a parchment-lined baking sheet. Gather the scraps, reshape them, and pat out the dough to a ½-inch thickness. Cut out as above.

12. Discard any remaining scrap or roll them into a "snake" to bake alongside the cut biscuits.

13. Bake 15 to 17 minutes, rotating the pan once halfway through, until the tops are golden brown. Serve immediately.

# Storing Your Biscuits

*Biscuits are best served warm from the oven, or at least the day they are* baked. But that doesn't mean you can't store them for a rainy day of stress eating later. Left out at room temperature, they are good for 1 or 2 days; reheat for best results.

Even better, biscuits can be stored in the fridge or the freezer to maximize their shelf life and conserve their freshness and texture. Store them in an airtight container or resealable bag; you'll just want to squeeze the bag to release all air before sealing. Also, make sure the biscuits are completely cooled before storing to avoid trapping excess moisture; otherwise, they could become soggy or gummy. In an airtight container or resealable bag, baked biscuits can last for up to a week in the fridge.

To freeze, individually wrap each biscuit in plastic wrap before placing in a freezer bag or airtight container for up to 3 months.

You can also freeze your unbaked biscuit dough rounds or squares for later baking. After cutting out your biscuits, arrange them on a parchment paper–lined baking sheet and cover with plastic wrap. Freeze them first on the baking sheet, then transfer them to an airtight container or freezer bag for storage.

# 2.
# HOW TO
# BE BASIC

*Base Biscuit Recipes*

# Patience and Persistence

My first biscuit-baking attempt was a disaster. In my defense, I was eight or nine—at the most. I added so much shortening and butter that the mixture boiled over the baking sheet and dripped onto Granny's oven floor. The smoke alarm went off before the timer did, and Granny came running into the kitchen with a broom and waving a towel. Clearly, she thought there would be more than a biscuit mishap to greet her as she turned the corner. Nope, just me and a burned pan of dough rocks.

However, Granny took those burnt biscuits out of the oven, grabbed some orange marmalade, and sat down and ate them. They were absolutely terrible. She told me not to give up and to keep trying until those biscuits turned out how I wanted them to. Everything in life takes patience and persistence, and sometimes a fire extinguisher.

Granny Geraldine used each experience in the kitchen to share a story or a lesson. On the day of my high school graduation, she gave me "one last present" wrapped in gold paper. It was a cookbook written by Cleora Butler, titled *Cleora's Kitchen*, the first one I'd own.

Born in 1901, Cleora was a beloved chef and caterer from Oklahoma. Her cookbook chronicles eight decades of cooking and tells the history of African American settlements in the Midwest and what life was like as a child on the wagon trails.

One of the recipes opens with Cleora telling the story of her first attempt at cooking. She was only ten but "determined to strike out on her own." She talks about the new baking powder her mother started using, Calumet, and the little booklet of recipes that accompanied it, one being for biscuits. It's the one Cleora used to impress her family. Unlike my first biscuits, her attempt was a success, and you can feel the affection she has for her family just by reading this story. According to Granny, she found the book at a thrift shop and thought I would enjoy making the connection and maybe even bake better biscuits. The shade! But she was right. Years later, I was able to find the 1911 Calumet baking powder recipe booklet that Cleora would have used to make those biscuits. It's become one of my most prized possessions.

# Baking Powder Biscuits

**YIELD: 10 TO 12 BISCUITS**

2½ cups / 300 grams
    all-purpose flour, plus extra
    for folding and cutting
1 tablespoon baking powder
2 teaspoons kosher salt
½ stick (4 tablespoons)
    unsalted butter, cold
2 cups full-fat buttermilk, cold
3 tablespoons melted salted
    butter

Joyce White's 1998 cookbook is filled with beautiful stories and recipes that feel as though they were pulled from my own childhood surrounded by southern church ladies. When she moved to New York from a small town in Alabama, she yearned for the food of her southern roots. By visiting local African American churches in Harlem and Bedford-Stuyvesant, White found both fellowship and the comfort of the home cooking she'd longed for.

This is a great recipe that comes together quickly. These biscuits rely on the heat activating the baking powder to produce a nice rise in the oven. Buttermilk adds a tang, elevating these simple biscuits. Brush the biscuits with melted butter as they come out of the oven to really set them off.

1. Adjust the oven rack to the middle position and preheat the oven to 450°F.

2. Place the flour, baking powder, and salt into a large bowl and whisk to combine.

3. Using the slicing side of a box grater, slice the butter into the flour mixture. Toss the sheets of butter in the flour and then lightly work the butter pieces between your fingers or use a pastry cutter to break them up and coat them with flour. Stop when the dough resembles coarse sand and there are still some small visible pieces of butter.

4. Place the biscuit mixture into the freezer for 15 minutes.

5. Add the buttermilk and gently stir with a spatula until the dough forms into a ball and no dry bits of flour are visible. The dough will be shaggy and sticky.

6. Turn the dough onto a lightly floured surface and lightly dust with flour. With floured hands, pat the dough into a ½-inch-thick 11 × 6-inch rectangle. Fold the ends of the rectangle toward the center, one end on top of the other, to create a trifold. Dust the top lightly with flour, press out to the same size rectangle again, and repeat the folding. Repeat this process a third time. After the third folding, pat the dough to a ½-inch thickness and cut out the biscuits using a floured 2½-inch biscuit cutter. Be careful to press straight down and do not twist the cutter.

7. Place the biscuit rounds 1 inch apart on a parchment-lined baking sheet. Gather the scraps, reshape them, and pat the dough out to ½-inch thickness. Cut out as above. Discard any remaining scraps.

8. Bake for 15 to 20 minutes, rotating the pan once halfway through, until the tops are golden brown. Brush tops with melted butter. Serve immediately.

# Angel Biscuits

**YIELD: 15 TO 18 BISCUITS**

2 cups full-fat buttermilk,
    warmed to 110°F

4½ teaspoons active dry yeast

2 tablespoons sugar

5 cups / 600 grams all-purpose
    flour, plus extra for folding
    and cutting

2 teaspoons baking powder

1½ teaspoons kosher salt

1 teaspoon baking soda

½ cup (96 grams) vegetable
    shortening, cold, broken into
    pea-sized pieces

1 stick (8 tablespoons) unsalted
    butter, cold

Angel biscuits use yeast in addition to baking powder to give them a little extra lift and fluff. They pop up tall, almost like those biscuits you buy in the can. We're going to leave behind those canned biscuits, though, because I was taught the only thing that should come out of a can is paint.

This recipe calls for letting the dough rest for about 30 minutes before folding and cutting out the biscuits. The rest gives the liquid more time to hydrate the flour and the yeast time to ferment, filling the dough with gas that will give these biscuits an airy texture. Angel biscuits make great dinner roll substitutes. I serve them more often during the holidays and at big family gatherings with just a slather of butter across the top.

1. Adjust the oven rack to the middle position and preheat the oven to 450°F.

2. Place the buttermilk, yeast, and sugar into a small bowl and stir gently to combine. Set aside until bubbles form on the surface of the mixture, 3 to 4 minutes.

3. Place the flour, baking powder, salt, and baking soda in a large bowl and whisk to combine. Scatter the pieces of shortening over the flour mixture.

4. Using the slicing side of a box grater, slice the butter into the flour mixture. Toss the sheets of butter in the flour and then lightly work the butter pieces between your fingers or use a pastry cutter to break them up and coat them with flour. Stop when the dough resembles coarse sand and there are still some small visible pieces of butter.

5. Make a well in the center of the mixture. Add the buttermilk mixture and stir gently with a spatula until the dough forms into a ball and no dry bits of flour are visible. The dough will be shaggy and sticky.

6. Cover with plastic wrap and set aside to rest in a warm, dry place for 30 minutes.

*Recipe continues*

7. Turn the dough onto a lightly floured surface and lightly dust with flour. This dough is easier to shape using a rolling pin. With floured hands, pat the dough into a ½-inch-thick 11 × 6-inch rectangle. Fold the ends of the rectangle toward the center, one end on top of the other, to create a trifold. Dust the top lightly with flour, press out to the same size rectangle again, and repeat the folding. Repeat this process a third time. After the third folding, pat the dough to a ½-inch thickness and cut out the biscuits using a floured 2-inch biscuit cutter. Be careful to press straight down and do not twist the cutter.

8. Place the biscuit rounds 1 inch apart on a parchment-lined baking sheet. Gather the scraps, reshape them, and pat the dough out to a ½-inch thickness. Cut out as above. Discard any remaining scraps.

9. Bake 15 to 20 minutes, rotating the pan once halfway through, until the tops are golden brown.

# Touch of Grace Biscuits

**YIELD: 6 BISCUITS**

2½ cups / 300 grams all-purpose flour, plus extra for folding and cutting

1 tablespoon baking powder

1½ teaspoons kosher salt

½ teaspoon baking soda

6 tablespoons vegetable shortening, cold, cut into ½-inch chunks

1¼ cups full-fat buttermilk, cold

3 tablespoons salted butter, melted (for brushing the tops of the biscuits, optional)

This style of biscuit is often referred to as "touch of grace" biscuits. The process for making them requires no extra tools such as a rolling pin or biscuit cutter. Your hands do all the work, tossing in the shortening, mixing in the buttermilk, pinching off large pieces of dough, shaping the rounds, then placing them in the skillet or on the sheet pan. This requires a "touch of grace." That grace flows through to your finished product: light and fluffy biscuits, large as a cat's head and wonderful for sandwiching a piece of salt-cured ham. These are the biscuits that, for me, resemble the texture and taste of the much-loved gas station biscuits. Gas stations with fresh biscuits are harder to find now. Back in the day, we would pass several as Granny and I drove down Highway 70 from Durham to Goldsboro, North Carolina. Only plain Neese's sausage for her and a juicy piece of country ham on a biscuit for me.

While I have little doubt that y'all have the "touch of grace," the recipe below does call for utensils to keep it a little less messy. When you fold in the buttermilk, you will notice that the texture of these biscuits is a little stickier than the typical rolled biscuit.

1. Adjust the oven rack to the middle position and preheat the oven to 475°F.

2. Place the flour, baking powder, salt, and baking soda in a large bowl and whisk to combine.

3. Using your fingers, a pastry cutter, or a fork, work the shortening into the flour mixture until the mixture resembles coarse sand. Make a well in the center of the flour mixture and add the buttermilk. Gently fold in the buttermilk with a spatula until no dry bits of flour are visible. The dough will be shaggy and sticky.

4. Turn the dough onto a lightly floured surface and lightly dust with flour. With floured hands, pat the dough to about a 1-inch thickness. To form the biscuits, pinch off a large piece of dough, about the size of a large egg, and place the dough in a 9-inch cast-iron skillet or parchment-lined baking sheet. Pat out to a 1-inch-thick round. Repeat with the remaining dough, letting the rounds in the skillet touch each other. Brush the melted butter over the tops of each biscuit (if using).

5. Bake for 10 to 15 minutes, rotating the skillet once halfway through, until the tops are golden brown. Serve immediately.

## THERE'S BUTTER AND THERE'S MILK

As the years have gone by, I've found myself in the mix of more culinary events and festivals, meeting so many talented people along the way. Sometimes, however, a few characters give me pause. One time, a chef's main dish involved a biscuit. It was a very detailed dish that required a host of very special ingredients, one being a specific kind of buttermilk. But due to a mix-up, there either wasn't enough buttermilk or it was the wrong kind, and I watched as she slowly started to unravel at the thought of making an adjustment and using something else. One of the event volunteers offered to run to the store and grab more buttermilk, giving the chef time to walk around complaining about what was missing, the delay, and a host of other nonsense. When she made her way over to me, I'd already listened long enough. I mentioned there was a ton of whole milk in the walk-in cooler, suggesting that maybe she could use that to get started. She responded by telling me that I must not make a lot of biscuits if I'd suggest using whole milk.

*Well, all right, girl; do you.*

One of the most common questions when it comes to biscuits is: What if you can't find buttermilk?

Buttermilk is a thick, creamy, glorious liquid that binds everything from biscuits to chocolate cake, and according to ancient grandma folklore, it can heal brittle bones and broken hearts. However, there are several other liquids that add their own flavor and flare to a warm biscuit. Heavy cream adds more richness, resulting in a tender biscuit with a super-light texture. Kefir or yogurt will add a tangy, buttery mouthfeel like buttermilk. The following recipes are for biscuits you can whip up in a flash using everything but buttermilk.

# Food in the Fellowship Hall

*Whatever was served in those restaurants Jim Crow kept us out of; we had something much better spread out on tables at the church.* —Renita Dortch, my mother

Sundays were spent in a combination of three places: my grandmother's house on Slocumb Street, the sanctuary of her church about four blocks away, and depending on which Sunday it was—because First Sunday and Second Sunday were not the same—the fellowship hall of the very same church. The fellowship hall was essentially the church civic center. It hosted receptions, Sunday school, vacation Bible school in the summer, and on First Sundays, some of the best fried chicken you will ever eat. I vividly remember sitting at long tables draped in plastic tablecloths on cold metal folding chairs that my legs would stick to in the summer.

My granny, Geraldine, was a church "mother" personified. Feeding people was her ministry. She, along with the other ladies (and men) who served on the kitchen committee, manned the church kitchen as though it were a Michelin-star restaurant serving $600 tasting menus. The flow would resemble an assembly line, with the plates and silverware at the beginning and biscuits or rolls and drinks at the end. The drink dispensers would be wiped down so they wouldn't drip, because *Jesus don't like mess.* Desserts would be on a separate table altogether.

My grandmother made sure that I knew the origins of the sanctity of the church dinner and the undeniable impact it had on the Black community. Her devout belief in Sunday supper still lives deep within me.

Though not exclusive to Black churches, the Sunday church dinner was refined by African Americans in the South. The Black church, from its inception, has been the foundation of our community. During the fight for civil rights, the church was the mobilization epicenter for all social and political activities. One of the essential functions of the churches was to serve as meeting locations for organizing volunteers. Plate sales, Friday fish fries, bake sales, and the revered Sunday church dinners all helped fund the fight for equal rights. There was power in a pot of greens and freedom funded by fried chicken.

My love of food and fellowship was kindled by the people who nurtured and fed me at St. James AME Zion Church in Goldsboro, North Carolina. My longing to still feel the embrace of a vibrant Sunday dinner table led me to host Sunday suppers in my home when I moved to Atlanta. After several years, they grew into pop-ups, which grew into a restaurant.

*Still We Rise*

# Fellowship Hall Biscuits

**YIELD: 8 TO 10 BISCUITS**

2½ cups / 300 grams all-purpose flour, plus extra for folding and cutting
1 tablespoon baking powder
1½ teaspoons kosher salt
1 stick (8 tablespoons) unsalted butter, cold
1½ cups evaporated milk

Over the years at homes and at church gatherings across the country, particularly in the South, I have eaten herb biscuits, biscuits made with molasses and sweet potatoes, biscuits with bacon bits, biscuits filled with bits of ham and sausage, jelly biscuits, as well as puffy and flaky Angel Biscuits, which are made with both baking powder and yeast. Mama, especially whenever she was having church company, used to stir in little finely minced onion in the batter and then scatter the top with several pinches of grated sharp cheddar cheese.

—Joyce White, *Soul Food: Recipes and Reflections from African-American Churches*

In the past, the cost of butter and buttermilk made these ingredients more of a luxury than a necessity in biscuits and other baked goods. Most of the older cookbooks and cooks I referenced didn't automatically suggest these items were needed to make great biscuits. Common ingredients were instead likely to be lard and whole or canned milk, or maybe even water. Evaporated milk has always intrigued me. From its use as a brine for fried chicken to its role as an ingredient for biscuits, evaporated milk is an economical liquid substitute that plays a recurring role in a lot of my family's recipes from the late '50s and '60s. In these biscuits, evaporated milk acts as an enriching agent by adding both moisture and an intense milky flavor. They're incredibly tasty when smeared with pimento cheese.

1. Adjust the oven rack to the middle position and preheat the oven to 450°F.

2. Place the flour, baking powder, and salt into a large bowl and whisk to combine.

3. Using the slicing side of a box grater, slice the butter into the flour mixture and stir until the butter is well coated with the flour.

4. Add the evaporated milk and stir gently with a spatula until the dough forms into a ball and no dry bits of flour are visible. The dough will be shaggy and sticky.

5. Turn the dough onto a lightly floured surface and lightly dust with flour. With floured hands, pat the dough into a ½-inch-thick 11 × 6-inch rectangle. Fold the ends of the rectangle toward the center, one end on top of the other, to create a trifold. Dust the top lightly with flour, press out to the same size rectangle again, and repeat the folding. Repeat this process a third time. After the third folding, pat the dough to a ½-inch thickness and cut out the biscuits using a floured 2½-inch biscuit cutter. Be careful to press straight down and do not twist the cutter.

6. Place the biscuit rounds 1 inch apart on a parchment-lined baking sheet. Gather the scraps, reshape them, and pat the dough out again to a ½-inch thickness. Cut out as above. Discard any remaining scraps.

7. Bake 15 to 17 minutes, rotating the pan once halfway through, until the tops are golden brown. Serve immediately.

# Whole Milk Biscuits

**YIELD: 12 BISCUITS**

2½ cups / 300 grams
   all-purpose flour, plus extra
   for folding and cutting
1 tablespoon baking powder
1 teaspoon kosher salt
1¼ cups whole milk, cold
1 stick (8 tablespoons) unsalted
   butter, melted

In Sheila Ferguson's cookbook, *Soul Food: Classic Cuisine from the Deep South*, she introduces us to her Grandmother Battle. A photograph of Martha Virginia Bullock Battle, a sharp lady standing tall in a fur-trimmed coat and feathered hat, accompanies the story of her freshly baked biscuits. The recipe uses shortening and butter as well as milk (not buttermilk!), which inspired me to experiment with my own base biscuits.

Buttermilk is often considered the key to great biscuits. However, buttermilk was not always easy to come by. When I was growing up, biscuits were made with all kinds of milk and even water. So, I wanted to make sure to include recipes that give you great results without buttermilk. One method is to add butter to your milk. You see what I did there. Old-fashioned buttermilk, at least from what I can remember, had flecks of butter floating in it. In these biscuits, I take some whole milk and add the melted butter to it to produce those flecks of butter that get dispersed throughout the dough, creating pockets of steam in your biscuits and making them as light and fluffy as they should be. And since we're foregoing the acidic buttermilk, we're using baking powder as the leavening agent here, omitting the need for baking soda.

1. Adjust the oven rack to the middle position and preheat the oven to 450°F.

2. Place the flour, baking powder, and salt in a medium bowl and whisk to combine.

3. Place the chilled milk in a small bowl. Pour the melted butter, while still hot, into the cold milk. Gently stir until the butter forms small clumps and the mixture looks curdled.

4. Pour the milk mixture into the flour mixture and stir gently with a spatula until the dough forms into a ball and no dry bits of flour are visible. The dough will be shaggy and sticky.

5. Turn the dough onto a lightly floured surface and lightly dust with flour. With floured hands, pat the dough into a ½-inch-thick 11 × 6-inch rectangle. Fold the ends of the rectangle toward the center, one end on top of the other, to create a trifold. Dust the top lightly with flour, press out to the same size rectangle again, and repeat the folding. Repeat this process a third time. After the third folding, pat the dough to a ½-inch thickness and cut out the biscuits using a floured 2½-inch biscuit cutter. Be careful to press straight down and do not twist the cutter.

6. Place the biscuit rounds 1 inch apart on a parchment-lined baking sheet. Gather the scraps, reshape them, and pat the dough out to a ½-inch thickness. Cut out as above. Discard any remaining scraps.

7. Bake for 15 to 18 minutes, rotating the pan once halfway through, until the tops are golden brown. Serve immediately.

# A Date with a Dish

*Ebony* magazine was a staple in a lot of Black American households. Granny kept them stacked on the table in the back room, by her favorite reading chair, and on the nightstand next to her bed. Sometimes she would cut out the recipe columns to be used at a later date. When she passed away, my mom and I found lots of these recipe clippings in many separate places in Granny's house, some dating back to the early '50s. One of the recipes was credited to Freda DeKnight, who I learned was the first food editor of *Ebony*. DeKnight wrote a bestselling cookbook in the 1940s, originally titled *A Date with a Dish: A Cook Book of American Negro Recipes*. There are several editions of this book, later rebranded as *The Ebony Cookbook*. However, the original 1948 edition includes a section called the Collector's Corner, featuring short bios of all the Black home cooks, chefs, and caterers who inspired DeKnight. It is the most phenomenal part of the book and has been left out of all the subsequent editions, similar to how DeKnight herself is too often left out of conversations about food journalism. Freda DeKnight was born in Topeka, Kansas, in 1909 and grew up in South Dakota. Her cookbook and Cleora Butler's were the first that I'd seen written by African Americans that did not focus on southern cooking. She makes note of this in the preface of her book:

> It is a fallacy, long disproved, that Negro cooks, chefs, caterers and homemakers can adapt themselves only to the standard Southern dishes, such as fried chicken, greens, corn pone and hot breads. Like other Americans living in various sections of the country they have naturally shown a desire to become versatile in the preparation of any dish, whether it is Spanish, Italian, French, Balinese or East Indian in origin.

Her presence can be felt in my best dishes, from my steak marinade to my hollandaise sauce over roasted cauliflower to, of course, my biscuits as well. There are nine biscuit recipes in *A Date with a Dish*. From southern yeast biscuits to lemon biscuits, they are all top tier. Her advice to "garnish the top of your biscuits with cranberries and/or dates" is what got me thinking outside the typical biscuit box to create some of the recipes in this book. In another recipe, keeping it simple, her sour cream biscuits have you melt shortening or butter and mix it with sour cream.

# Sour Cream Biscuits

YIELD: 12 TO 14 BISCUITS

2½ cups / 300 grams
all-purpose flour, plus extra
for folding and cutting
1 tablespoon baking powder
2 teaspoons kosher salt
½ teaspoon baking soda
1½ cups full-fat buttermilk, cold
½ cup sour cream, cold

Biscuits are always better with some fat added to the mix. Butter is my usual go-to; however, there are some elite substitutions, such as sour cream, which adds moisture and a creamy, buttery tang to these biscuits.

1. Adjust the oven rack to the middle position and preheat the oven to 450°F.

2. Place the flour, baking powder, salt, and baking soda in a large bowl and whisk to combine.

3. Place the buttermilk and sour cream in a small bowl and whisk to combine.

4. Add the buttermilk mixture to the flour mixture and, using a spatula, stir until the dough forms into a ball and no dry bits of flour are visible. The dough will be shaggy and sticky.

5. Turn the dough onto a lightly floured surface and lightly dust with flour. With floured hands, pat the dough into a ½-inch-thick 11 × 6-inch rectangle. Fold the ends of the rectangle toward the center, one on top of the other, to create a trifold. Dust the top lightly with flour, pat the dough to a ½-inch thickness, Dust lightly again with flour, press out to the same size rectangle again, and repeat the folding. Repeat this process a third time. After the third folding, pat the dough to a ½-inch thickness and cut out the biscuits using a floured 2½-inch biscuit cutter. Be careful to press straight down and do not twist the cutter.

6. Place the biscuit rounds 1 inch apart on a parchment-lined baking sheet. Gather the scraps, reshape them, and pat the dough out to a ½-inch thickness. Cut out as above. Discard any remaining scraps.

7. Bake 10 to 12 minutes, rotating the pan once halfway through, until the tops are golden brown. Serve immediately.

# Yogurt Biscuits

**YIELD: 15 OR 16 BISCUITS**

3 cups / 360 grams all-purpose
  flour, plus extra for folding
  and cutting
2 tablespoons baking powder
1 teaspoon kosher salt
½ teaspoon baking soda
1 stick (8 tablespoons) salted
  butter, cold
3 cups plain full-fat Greek
  yogurt, cold

Yogurt does a lot of heavy lifting in my house. We use it as the base for sauces and spreads—but for biscuits? Absolutely. Yogurt isn't that different from today's commercial buttermilk, which is cultured to produce that acidic tang that yogurt also has. The yogurt activates the baking soda, helping these biscuits to rise and making them light and fluffy.

1. Adjust the oven rack to the middle position and preheat the oven to 450°F.

2. Place the flour, baking powder, salt, and baking soda in a large bowl and whisk to combine. Grate the butter using the slicing side of a box grater. Scatter the butter over the flour and toss to coat. Add the yogurt and, using a spatula or wooden spoon, fold the yogurt into the mixture until the dough forms a ball and no dry bits of flour are visible. The dough will be shaggy and sticky.

3. Turn the dough onto a lightly floured surface and lightly dust with flour. With floured hands, pat the dough into a ½-inch-thick 11 × 6-inch rectangle. Fold the ends of the rectangle toward the center, one end on top of the other, to create a trifold. Dust the top lightly with flour and press out to the same size rectangle again and repeat the folding. Repeat this a third time. After the third fold, pat the dough to ½-inch thickness and cut out the biscuits using a 2½-inch biscuit cutter. Be careful to press straight down and do not twist the cutter.

4. Place the biscuit rounds 1 inch apart on a parchment-lined baking sheet. Gather the scraps, reshape, and pat out to ½-inch thickness and cut out as above. Discard any remaining scraps.

5. Bake for 15 to 18 minutes, rotating the pan once halfway through, until the tops are golden brown. Serve immediately.

## UNBUTTERED AND UNBOTHERED

We shred pounds of butter each day at our little biscuit eatery. It's delivered by the case each week, but as the business grows, we seem to run out quicker than it comes. Butter was once a treasured luxury that most of the cooks in my family used sparingly, reserving it for cakes and using softened butter for the dinner table to "season" your breads and vegetables. So, biscuits were often made with several other fats to produce the flakiest of layers.

Each kind of fat brings its own distinctive flavor to each batch of biscuits. Fats such as bacon grease and duck fat all carry their own essence, creating a unique taste with each bite.

Here are a few ways to roll out your next batch of biscuits using different types of fat. Hold that butter off to the side, and instead use it to slather across the tops when they are fresh out of the oven.

# Duck Fat Biscuits

**YIELD: 10 TO 12 BISCUITS**

2½ cups / 300 grams all-purpose flour, plus extra for folding and cutting
1 tablespoon baking powder
1½ teaspoons kosher salt
½ teaspoon baking soda
½ cup duck fat, cold
1 cup full-fat buttermilk, cold

In North Carolina, we have a dish called chicken pastry or chicken and pastry, depending on what your grandma called it. It is remarkably like chicken and dumplings, which is often made by adding what is basically drop biscuit dough to the stew. The "pastry" uses chicken fat in the dough, which gives it great flavor.

One Christmas, I thought I would be fancy and make a cassoulet with biscuit dumplings on top. Inspired by the chicken fat biscuit dumpling method, I subbed in duck fat. To keep it real with y'all, the cassoulet part of the dish wasn't the most popular, but the overwhelming, rich duck fat biscuits received high praise. The duck fat lends a tender, flaky texture and produces a biscuit with a nice golden top and great, slightly sweet flavor.

1. Adjust the oven rack to the middle position and preheat the oven to 450°F.

2. Place the flour, baking powder, salt, and baking soda in a large bowl and whisk to combine.

3. Using your fingers, work the duck fat into the flour mixture until only pea-sized pieces of duck fat remain.

4. Add the buttermilk and stir gently with a spatula until the dough forms into a ball and no dry bits of flour are visible. The dough will be shaggy and sticky.

5. Turn the dough onto a lightly floured surface and lightly dust with flour. With floured hands, pat the dough into a ½-inch-thick 11 × 6-inch rectangle. Fold the ends of the rectangle toward the center, one end on top of the other, to create a trifold. Dust the top lightly with flour, press out to the same size rectangle again, and repeat the folding. Repeat this process a third time. After the third folding, pat the dough to a ½-inch thickness and cut out the biscuits using a floured 2½-inch biscuit cutter. Be careful to press straight down and do not twist the cutter.

6. Place the biscuit rounds 1 inch apart on a parchment-lined baking sheet. Gather the scraps, reshape them, and pat the dough out to a ½-inch thickness. Cut out as above. Discard any remaining scraps.

7. Bake for 10 to 12 minutes, rotating the pan once halfway through, until the tops are golden brown. Serve immediately.

# Duke's Mayo Biscuits

**YIELD: 12 BISCUITS**

3 cups / 360 grams all-purpose
flour, plus extra for folding
and cutting
1 tablespoon baking powder
1 teaspoon kosher salt
½ teaspoon baking soda
½ cup Duke's mayonnaise
1 cup full-fat buttermilk, cold

The practice of adding mayonnaise to cakes is often traced to the Depression era, when certain staple items such as eggs, milk, and butter were rationed. Since mayonnaise consists of egg yolks, oil, lemon juice, vinegar, and spices, it was used as a substitute for fresh eggs and fat. And since it's mainly oil, it adds a moist and tender texture to biscuits, and the little bit of acid it contains assists in making those biscuits rise. Duke's mayonnaise is my secret ingredient in everything from buttery golden grilled cheese to scrambled eggs to—now you know—biscuits. If you cannot find Duke's in your area, you can substitute another brand such as Hellmann's or Best Foods.

1. Adjust the oven rack to the middle position and preheat the oven to 450°F.

2. Place the flour, baking powder, salt, and baking soda in a large bowl and whisk to combine.

3. Add the mayonnaise and stir gently with a spatula until combined and no large clumps of mayonnaise remain. Add the buttermilk and stir gently until the dough forms into a ball and no dry bits of flour are visible. The dough will be shaggy and sticky.

4. Turn the dough onto a lightly floured surface and lightly dust with flour. With floured hands, pat the dough into a ½-inch-thick 11 × 6-inch rectangle. Fold the ends of the rectangle toward the center, one end on top of the other, to create a trifold. Dust the top lightly with flour, press out to the same size rectangle again, and repeat the folding. Repeat this process a third time. After the third folding, pat the dough to a ½-inch thickness and cut out the biscuits using a floured 3½-inch biscuit cutter. Be careful to press straight down and do not twist the cutter.

5. Place the biscuit rounds 1 inch apart on a parchment-lined baking sheet. Gather the scraps, reshape them, and pat the dough out to a ½-inch thickness. Cut out as above. Discard any remaining scraps.

6. Bake 15 to 20 minutes, rotating the pan once halfway through, until the tops are golden brown. Serve immediately.

# Heavy Cream Biscuits

**YIELD: 8 TO 10 BISCUITS**

2 cups / 240 grams all-purpose
   flour, plus extra for folding
   and cutting
1 tablespoon baking powder
1½ teaspoons kosher salt
1½ cups heavy cream, cold
2 tablespoons salted butter,
   melted (optional)

Heavy cream, also referred to as heavy whipping cream, has the highest fat content of the dairy products not named butter, with at least 36 to 40 percent milk fat. It's one of the most versatile ingredients you can have in your fridge, used in everything from ice creams to pasta sauces to biscuits. These cream biscuits are a great base recipe that I often elevate with the addition of fresh herbs or fruits. The milk-fat component of the heavy cream produces the fluffiest of biscuits with an incredible texture. They are perfect to use for shortcake recipes such as strawberry or apple. (Since these are on the lighter side, they are not sturdy enough for hearty sandwiches, like a fried chicken biscuit.)

With all that cream, the only butter needed for this recipe is an optional brush across the tops before serving. Or if you're like me, you could dip your biscuits in a bowl of melted butter while stress eating the whole pan as you try to meet your cookbook deadlines.

1. Adjust the oven rack to the middle position and preheat the oven to 475°F.

2. Place the flour, baking powder, and salt in a medium bowl and whisk to combine. Make a well in the center of the flour mixture and pour in the heavy cream. Using a spatula, slowly stir the cream into the flour until the dough forms into a ball.

3. Turn the dough onto a lightly floured surface and lightly dust with flour. With floured hands, pat the dough into a ½-inch-thick 11 × 6-inch rectangle. You may use a rolling pin to roll the dough out if necessary. Fold the ends of the rectangle toward the center, one end on top of the other, to create a trifold. Dust the top lightly with flour, press out to the same size rectangle again, and repeat the folding. Repeat this process a third time. After the third folding, pat the dough to a ½-inch thickness and cut out the biscuits using a floured 2½-inch biscuit cutter. Be careful to press straight down and do not twist the cutter.

4. Place the biscuit rounds 1 inch apart on a parchment-lined baking sheet. Gather the scraps, reshape them, and pat them out to a ½-inch thickness. Cut out as above. Discard any remaining scraps.

5. Bake 15 to 20 minutes, rotating the pan once halfway through, until the tops are golden brown. Remove from the oven and brush the tops with the melted butter (if using). Serve immediately.

*Still We Rise*

# Lard Biscuits

**YIELD: 10 TO 12 BISCUITS**

2½ cups / 300 grams all-
    purpose flour, plus extra for
    folding and cutting
1 tablespoon baking powder
1½ teaspoons kosher salt
½ teaspoon baking soda
½ cup rendered lard, cold
1 cup full-fat buttermilk, cold

Lard can be substituted for butter in most baking recipes. It's my ideal baking fat for biscuits and pies due to the depth of flavor it lends to baked goods. Since it's 100 percent fat, lard adds a higher degree of tenderization than butter, and lard's larger fat crystals give biscuits a flaky texture. If you can get your hands on leaf lard, then I recommend using that for this recipe. If not, no need to worry; other forms of rendered lard will still produce superior results. These biscuits bake up on the softer side, making them ideal to eat with just a dollop of jam or soft cheese or butter.

1. Adjust the oven rack to the middle position and preheat the oven to 450°F.

2. Place the flour, baking powder, salt, and baking soda in a large bowl and whisk to combine.

3. Using your fingers, work the lard into the flour mixture until only pea-sized pieces of lard remain. Add the buttermilk and stir gently with a spatula until the dough forms into a ball and no dry bits of flour are visible. The dough will be shaggy and sticky.

4. Turn the dough onto a lightly floured surface and lightly dust with flour. With floured hands, pat the dough into a ½-inch-thick 11 × 6-inch rectangle. Fold the ends of the rectangle toward the center, one end on top of the other, to create a trifold. Dust the top lightly with flour, press out to the same size rectangle again, and repeat the folding. Repeat this process a third time. After the third folding, pat the dough to a ½-inch thickness and cut out the biscuits using a floured 2½-inch biscuit cutter. Be careful to press straight down and do not twist the cutter.

5. Place the biscuit rounds 1 inch apart on a parchment-lined baking sheet. Gather the scraps, reshape them, and pat the dough out to a ½-inch thickness. Cut out as above. Discard any remaining scraps.

6. Bake for 10 to 12 minutes, rotating the pan once halfway through, until the tops are golden brown. Serve immediately.

# 3.
# RISE TO NEW HEIGHTS

*Other Ways to Shape, Cut, and Bake Up a Biscuit*

# Drop Biscuits

**YIELD: 8 TO 10 BISCUITS**

2 cups / 240 grams all-purpose
    flour
2 teaspoons baking powder
1 teaspoon sugar
¾ teaspoon kosher salt
½ teaspoon baking soda
1¼ cups full-fat buttermilk, cold
1 stick (8 tablespoons)
    unsalted butter, melted, plus
    2 tablespoons for brushing

Drop biscuits have the same chemical makeup as my go-to rolled buttermilk biscuit (The Bomb Buttermilk Biscuit, page 33), using both baking powder and baking soda. However, we're opting to use a ¼-cup measure to scoop and drop the dough onto a baking sheet instead of rolling and cutting out the biscuits. Drop biscuits are coarser in appearance and texture and have a crunchy exterior that makes them great with gravy.

1. Adjust the oven rack to the middle position and preheat the oven to 450°F. Line a baking sheet with parchment paper and lightly grease it with cooking spray.

2. Place the flour, baking powder, sugar, salt, and baking soda in a large bowl and whisk to combine.

3. Place the buttermilk and warm melted butter in a small bowl and stir until the butter forms small clumps and the mixture looks curdled (you should see bits of butter throughout). Add the buttermilk mixture to the flour mixture and stir gently with a rubber spatula just until the ingredients are incorporated and the mixture pulls away slightly from the edges of the bowl.

4. Using a greased ¼-cup measure, scoop the dough onto the prepared baking sheet, 1 inch apart.

5. Bake for 15 to 17 minutes, rotating the pan once halfway through, until the tops are golden brown. Remove from the oven and brush with the remaining 2 tablespoons melted butter. Serve warm.

*Cook's Note: Spraying the scoop or measuring cup with cooking spray will prevent the drop biscuit dough from sticking to the scoop while you portion out the biscuits.*

# Pretzel Biscuits

YIELD: 6 BISCUITS

## BISCUITS

2½ cups / 300 grams
    all-purpose flour, plus extra
    for folding and cutting
1 tablespoon baking powder
1½ teaspoons kosher salt
½ teaspoon baking soda
2 tablespoons (27 grams)
    vegetable shortening, cold,
    cut into ½-inch chunks
1 stick (8 tablespoons) unsalted
    butter, cold
1½ cups full-fat buttermilk, cold

## PRETZEL WASH

1½ teaspoons baking soda
1 egg beaten with 1 teaspoon
    water
Pretzel or coarse salt, for
    sprinkling

My son, Charlie, is a lover of both pretzels and biscuits. Once, I attempted to make pretzels from scratch, and while they turned out better than expected, they just took too long to make. So, one day I rolled the dice, took some of the ingredients and steps from a pretzel recipe, and added them to biscuits. The results were too legit to quit, and these have become my go-to when I want to flex my Jedi biscuit-baking skills. The baking soda wash adds a golden top that's crisp and crunchy when you bite into it, and the biscuit tastes like a tangy, well-buttered salty cracker with a soft interior. This is Charlie's favorite flavor biscuit. I have no doubt you'll love it just as much.

These biscuits are best eaten the day they are baked. If you wait until the next day to eat them, the tops get slightly soggy from the baking soda wash. And if egg isn't your thing, feel free to omit the egg wash. It does give the biscuits a nice gloss, but it's not mandatory for this recipe.

1. Adjust the oven rack to the middle position and preheat the oven to 450°F.

2. For the biscuits: Place the flour, baking powder, salt, and baking soda in a large bowl and whisk to combine.

3. Using your fingers, a pastry cutter, or a fork, work the shortening into the flour mixture until only pea-sized pieces of shortening remain. Using the slicing side of a box grater, slice the butter into the flour mixture. Toss the sheets of butter in the flour and then lightly work the butter pieces between your fingers or use a pastry cutter to break them up and coat them with flour. Stop when the dough resembles coarse sand and there are still some small visible pieces of butter.

4. Place the biscuit mixture into the freezer for 15 minutes.

5. Add the buttermilk and stir gently with a spatula until the dough forms into a ball and no dry bits of flour are visible. The dough will be shaggy and sticky.

*Recipe continues*

6. Turn the dough onto a lightly floured surface and lightly dust with flour. With floured hands, pat the dough into a ½-inch-thick 11 × 6-inch rectangle. Fold the ends of the rectangle toward the center, one end on top of the other, to create a trifold. Dust the top lightly with flour, press out to the same size rectangle again, and repeat the folding. Repeat this process a third time. After the third folding, pat the dough to a ½-inch thickness and cut out the biscuits using a floured 3½-inch biscuit cutter. Be careful to press straight down and do not twist the cutter.

7. Place the biscuit rounds 1 inch apart on a parchment-lined baking sheet. Gather the scraps, reshape them, and pat the dough out to a ½-inch thickness. Cut out as above. Discard any remaining scraps.

8. For the pretzel wash: In a small saucepan, bring ½ cup water to a boil and slowly stir in the baking soda. The mixture should start to foam. Remove from the heat and continue stirring until the foam subsides. Brush the tops of each biscuit with the warm soda wash.

9. Brush the egg wash over the soda wash for the perfect golden-brown glow. Sprinkle with salt and bake for 15 to 17 minutes, rotating the pan once halfway through, until the tops are golden brown. Serve immediately.

# Butter Swim Biscuits

YIELD: 9 TO 10 BISCUITS

1 stick (8 tablespoons) unsalted
    butter
2½ cups / 300 grams all-
    purpose flour
2 tablespoons kosher salt
4 teaspoons baking powder
1 tablespoon sugar
2 cups full-fat buttermilk,
    room temperature

Butter swim biscuits are made by letting buttermilk biscuit dough literally swim in a pool of melted butter. Butter swims are close to my favorite way to bake biscuits, mainly because they defy all the cardinal "rules" that one MUST supposedly follow to master the perfect biscuit. You don't need very cold or frozen butter; you can even use room-temperature buttermilk. The dough is mixed in one bowl as your butter melts in a cast-iron skillet (a baking dish will also suffice), and then you pour the biscuit batter over the melted butter. The biscuit dough will look like over-oiled focaccia, but don't worry, the butter will bake right into that batter, giving you crispy-crust biscuits with soft and fluffy interiors. Call it buttery bliss in a baking dish. Now say that five times fast.

1. Adjust the oven rack to the middle position and preheat the oven to 450°F. Place the butter into a 9-inch cast-iron skillet or a 9 × 9-inch casserole dish and set inside the oven while it is preheating.

2. Place the flour, salt, baking powder, and sugar in a large bowl and whisk to combine. Add the buttermilk and stir gently with a spatula just until combined. Do not overmix.

3. Remove the hot cast-iron skillet from the oven and gently pour the batter over the melted butter. Use a knife or spatula to spread the dough evenly in the skillet.

4. Run a knife through the dough, "cutting" it into 3-inch squares right in the skillet.

5. Bake for 20 to 25 minutes, rotating the pan once halfway through, until the tops of the biscuits are golden brown. Serve immediately.

# Pull-Apart Biscuits

YIELD: 12 TO 14 BISCUITS, DEPENDING ON HOW CLOSELY YOU CUT THEM TO EACH OTHER

2½ cups / 300 grams all-purpose flour, plus extra for folding and cutting

1 tablespoon baking powder

1¼ teaspoons kosher salt

½ teaspoon baking soda

2 tablespoons vegetable shortening, cold, cut into ½-inch chunks

1 stick (8 tablespoons) unsalted butter, cold, cut into ⅛-inch slices

1¾ cups full-fat buttermilk, cold

These biscuits are one of my most shared on social media. Apparently, leaving the edges on the biscuits while they bake is both genius and bizarre, and will have you going viral on TikTok even when you don't have a TikTok account. I have eaten biscuits in many styles, including rolled, dropped, and burned to hell and back. Then there are pull-apart (a.k.a. sheet-pan) biscuits, although these can also be baked in a cast-iron skillet. After patting out the dough, you place it on the sheet pan, press the biscuit cutter gently into the dough to leave an indentation in the shape of a biscuit, and then bake. After baking, you can pull apart the biscuit rounds, which come out with the softest edges. As for the surrounding baked biscuit scraps, well, these are used as spoons for jelly and gravy and were always given to the kids.

1. Adjust the oven rack to the middle position and preheat the oven to 450°F.

2. Place the flour, baking powder, salt, and baking soda in a large bowl and whisk to combine.

3. Using your fingers, a pastry cutter, or a fork, work the shortening into the flour mixture until only pea-sized pieces of shortening remain. Toss the butter slices into the flour, and then lightly work the butter pieces between your fingers or use a pastry cutter to break them up and coat them with flour. Stop when the dough resembles coarse sand and there are still some small visible pieces of butter.

4. Place the biscuit mixture into the freezer for 15 minutes.

5. Slowly add the buttermilk and stir gently with a spatula until the dough forms into a ball and no dry bits of flour are visible. The dough will be shaggy and sticky.

6. Turn the dough onto a lightly floured surface and lightly dust with flour. With floured hands, pat the dough into a ½-inch-thick 11 × 6-inch rectangle. Fold the ends of the rectangle toward the center, one end on top of the other, to create a trifold. Dust the top lightly with flour, press it out to the same size rectangle again, and repeat the folding. Repeat this process a third time.

7. Gently lift the dough "sheet" (with your hands or a bench scraper to assist) and place it on a parchment-lined baking sheet. Press it out to a ½-inch thickness, about 12 × 8½ inches.

8. Cut the dough into rounds using a floured 2½-inch biscuit cutter. Be careful to press straight down and do not twist the cutter to leave an indentation of the biscuit round. Do not move the rounds or the scraps from the pan.

9. Bake for 15 to 17 minutes, rotating the pan once halfway through, until the tops are golden brown. Serve the rounds and "scraps" warm.

*Still We Rise*

# Gluten-Free Biscuits You'll Actually Want to Eat

**YIELD: 8 TO 10 BISCUITS**

2½ cups / 398 grams gluten-free flour, plus extra for folding and cutting (see Cook's Note)

2 teaspoons arrowroot starch

1 tablespoon baking powder

1½ teaspoons kosher salt

½ teaspoon baking soda

1 stick (8 tablespoons) unsalted butter, frozen

3 tablespoons plain full-fat Greek yogurt, cold

1¼ cups full-fat buttermilk, cold

*Cook's Note: We used Cup4Cup Gluten Free Multipurpose Flour for this recipe, which you can purchase at some grocery stores and online.*

Everyone should be able to enjoy a good biscuit. But I understand, wheat is the mortal enemy for a lot of people. Several of them are close friends of mine. Like Chef Mary Schowe, who came to work with me a few years ago. She's an outstanding chef and a treasure trove of knowledge when it comes to everything from passing health inspections to working with gluten-free flours. So I immediately went to work trying to come up with a gluten-free buttermilk biscuit that tastes like something you would want to keep eating. Arrowroot starch works to bind the ingredients and helps create a lighter and fluffier texture that can be hard to achieve with gluten-free flours. The yogurt works to add even more moisture as well as to mask the gritty texture that xanthan gum can add.

1. Adjust the oven rack to the middle position and preheat the oven to 450°F.

2. Place the flour, arrowroot starch, baking powder, salt, and baking soda in a large bowl and whisk to combine.

3. Using the slicing side of a box grater, slice the butter into the flour mixture and toss to coat. Toss the sheets of butter in the flour, and then lightly work the butter pieces between your fingers or use a pastry cutter to break them up and coat them with flour. Stop when the dough resembles coarse sand and there are still some small visible pieces of butter. Place the biscuit mixture into the freezer for 15 minutes.

4. Add the yogurt and gently fold it into the flour mixture, just to combine. Add the buttermilk and stir gently with a spatula until the dough forms into a ball and no dry bits of flour are visible. The dough will be shaggy and sticky.

5. Turn the dough onto a lightly floured surface and lightly dust with flour. With floured hands, pat the dough into a ½-inch-thick 11 × 6-inch rectangle. Fold the ends of the rectangle toward the center, one end on top of the other, to create a trifold. Dust the top lightly with flour, press out to the same size rectangle again, and repeat the folding. Repeat this process a third time. After the third folding, pat the dough to a ½-inch thickness and cut out the biscuits using a floured 2½-inch biscuit cutter. Be careful to press straight down and do not twist the cutter.

6. Place the biscuit rounds 1 inch apart on a parchment-lined baking sheet. Gather the scraps, reshape them, and pat the dough out to a ½-inch thickness. Cut out as above. Discard any remaining scraps.

7. Bake for 15 to 20 minutes, rotating the pan once halfway through, until the tops are golden brown. Serve immediately.

# 4.
## IN THE MIX

*All—Purpose Biscuit Mix*

# All-Purpose Biscuit Mix

**YIELD: ABOUT 8¾ CUPS BISCUIT MIX (ABOUT 3 BATCHES OF BISCUITS)**

8 cups / 964 grams all-purpose flour
4 tablespoons baking powder
1½ tablespoons kosher salt
1 cup vegetable shortening, cold, cubed

In 1941, Lucille Bishop Smith published *Lucille's Treasure Chest of Fine Foods*, a cookbook that was a box set of recipe cards. A few years later, she developed an "all-purpose hot roll mix" for a church fundraiser that became such a success she was soon selling over two hundred cases a week at the general store near her husband's BBQ restaurant. Chili biscuits, bite-sized biscuits stuffed with chili, were Smith's signature dish, and they were served at the White House during Lyndon Johnson's presidency and on American Airlines flights. She was a true culinary pioneer. Her great-grandson, Chris Williams, opened a restaurant in her honor in Houston, Lucille's, where her legacy and chili biscuits live on. In this chapter, we'll honor Lucille Bishop Smith, baking up several flavors of biscuits, stacks of pancakes, and more, using an all-purpose mix.

Having an all-purpose baking mix on deck makes biscuit making a breeze. It's also great for things like pancakes, as we'll see later, but we'll stay on theme here. If you ever find yourself agreeing to making 1,500 biscuit sliders for a wedding brunch, I would highly advise you reconsider. However, one way to cut a corner and be ready to whip up biscuits anytime is to have a simple all-purpose mix in the fridge. When we need to bake up thousands of biscuits in a short amount of time, we can use the food processor to cut in the butter and shortening. Like for the wedding brunch that ends up needing 3,500 biscuits versus the original 1,500 requested. Might tell that story at some point.

1. Place the flour, baking powder, and salt into the bowl of a food processor and pulse for 10 to 15 seconds to combine.

2. Scatter the cubed shortening over the top of the flour mixture and pulse for 15 to 20 seconds, until well combined and the mixture resembles cornmeal.

3. Use immediately or store in an airtight container in the refrigerator for up to 3 months.

# Quick Buttermilk Biscuits

YIELD: 6 TO 8 BISCUITS

2½ cups / 368 grams
   All-Purpose Biscuit Mix
   (page 82)
1¼ cups full-fat buttermilk, cold
All-purpose flour, for folding
   and cutting
3 tablespoons salted butter,
   melted

Now that you have your biscuit mix chilling in the fridge, you'll want to crank out a few biscuits to show off. Here's a quick recipe to get biscuits on the table before your family wakes up or to make to enjoy by yourself in peace and quiet before everyone gets home. That's normally what I do.

1. Adjust the oven rack to the middle position and preheat the oven to 450°F.

2. Place the biscuit mix in a medium bowl and make a well in the center. Add the buttermilk and stir gently with a spatula until the dough forms into a ball and no dry bits of flour are visible. The dough will be shaggy and sticky.

3. Turn the dough onto a lightly floured surface and lightly dust with flour. With floured hands, pat the dough into a ½-inch-thick 11 × 6-inch rectangle. Fold the ends of the rectangle toward the center, one end on top of the other, to create a trifold. Dust the top lightly with flour, press out to the same size rectangle again, and repeat the folding. Repeat this process a third time. After the third folding, pat the dough to a ½-inch thickness and cut out the biscuits using a floured 2½-inch biscuit cutter.

4. Place the biscuit rounds 1 inch apart on a parchment-lined baking sheet. Gather the scraps, reshape them, and pat out to a ½-inch thickness. Cut out as above. Discard any remaining scraps.

5. Bake for 10 to 15 minutes, rotating the pan once halfway through, until the tops are golden brown. Brush the tops of warm biscuits with melted butter.

# Biscuit Mix Bis-cakes

**YIELD: 8 TO 10 PANCAKES**

2 cups / 295 grams All-Purpose
Biscuit Mix (page 82)

1 cup whole milk (you can also
try buttermilk)

2 large eggs

3 tablespoons sugar

2 tablespoons unsalted butter,
melted, plus more for
cooking

The great thing about the all-purpose mix is that it can be used in many recipes, from biscuits to pancakes and waffles, as a substitute for a store-bought mix. These pancakes come together in a flash and are soft and fluffy, with each bite melting in your mouth. Don't forget the syrup.

1. Place the biscuit mix, milk, eggs, sugar, and melted butter in a medium bowl, stirring until combined (lumps in pancake batter are totally OK).

2. Heat a skillet over medium heat or preheat your griddle to 350°F. Grease with melted butter or nonstick cooking spray. Pour or scoop the batter onto the prepared skillet, using approximately ¼ cup for each pancake.

3. Cook until surface bubbles start to appear and the edges are dry enough to get your spatula under, about 2 minutes. Flip and cook until lightly browned and cooked in the middle, another 1 to 2 minutes.

4. Serve immediately with syrup.

# 7UP Biscuits

**YIELD: 8 TO 10 BISCUITS**

2 tablespoons salted butter
2½ cups / 368 grams
  All-Purpose Biscuit Mix
  (page 82)
½ cup sour cream, cold
¾ cup 7UP or other lemon-lime
  soda, cold
All-purpose flour, for folding
  and cutting

These are soda biscuits, but not to be confused with *baking* soda. We're pouring 7UP into the batter, which makes for a high rise and light texture. The slight sweetness to these buttery biscuits makes them great for the purist who likes their biscuits with just a slather of honey. These are baked in a cast-iron skillet; a couple of tablespoons of melted salted butter are drizzled over the bottom of the skillet to make for a rich interior and a crisp crust.

1. Adjust the oven rack to the middle position and preheat the oven to 450°F.

2. Place the butter in a cast-iron skillet and set it in the preheating oven. Once the butter is melted, remove the skillet from the oven and set it aside.

3. Place the biscuit mix in a medium bowl and make a well in the center. Add the sour cream and, using a spatula, fold gently to incorporate. Make another well in the center and add the 7UP. Stir gently until the ingredients are combined, the dough forms into a ball, and no dry bits of flour are visible. The dough will be shaggy and sticky.

4. Turn the dough onto a lightly floured surface and lightly dust with flour. With floured hands, pat the dough into a ½-inch-thick 11 × 6-inch rectangle. Fold the ends of the rectangle toward the center, one end on top of the other, to create a trifold. Dust the top lightly with flour, press out to the same size rectangle again, and repeat the folding. Repeat this process a third time. After the third folding, pat the dough to a ½-inch thickness and cut out the biscuits using a floured 2½-inch biscuit cutter.

5. Place the biscuit rounds in the cast-iron skillet with the melted butter. Gather the scraps, reshape them, and pat the dough out to a ½-inch thickness. Cut out as above and place in skillet. Discard any remaining scraps.

6. Bake for 10 to 15 minutes, rotating the pan once halfway through, until the tops are golden brown.

# Cola Biscuits

**YIELD: 6 TO 8 BISCUITS**

½ stick (4 tablespoons) salted
   butter
2 cups / 295 grams All-Purpose
   Biscuit Mix (page 82)
2 tablespoons light brown
   sugar
½ cup sour cream, cold
½ cup cola, cold
All-purpose flour, for folding
   and cutting

These "soda" biscuits take on the dark sweetness of the cola and brown sugar. The recipe calls for light brown sugar, but you can substitute dark brown for an even richer molasses flavor. I've used cola biscuits as appetizers for gatherings with dollops of bacon jam sandwiched in between because . . . why not?!

1. Adjust the oven rack to the middle position and preheat the oven to 450°F.

2. Place the butter in a cast-iron skillet and set it in the preheating oven. Once the butter is melted, remove the skillet from the oven and set it aside.

3. Place the biscuit mix and brown sugar in a medium bowl and whisk to combine. Make a well in the center of the biscuit mix, add the sour cream and, using a spatula, fold gently to incorporate. Make another well in the center and add the cola. Stir gently until the ingredients are combined, the dough forms into a ball, and no dry bits of flour are visible. The dough will be shaggy and sticky.

4. Turn the dough onto a lightly floured surface and lightly dust with flour. With floured hands, pat the dough into a ½-inch-thick 11 × 6-inch rectangle. Fold the ends of the rectangle toward the center, one end on top of the other, to create a trifold. Dust the top lightly with flour, press out to the same size rectangle again, and repeat the folding. Repeat this process a third time. After the third folding, pat the dough to a ½-inch thickness and cut out the biscuits using a floured 2½-inch biscuit cutter.

5. Place the biscuit rounds in the cast-iron skillet with the melted butter so that they are touching. Gather the scraps, reshape them, and pat the dough out to a ½-inch thickness. Cut out as above and place in skillet. Discard any remaining scraps.

6. Bake for 10 to 15 minutes, rotating the pan once halfway through, until the tops are golden brown.

*Still We Rise*

# 5.
## SAVORY
## BISCUITS

# Everything "Bagel" Biscuits

YIELD: 6 TO 8 BISCUITS

## EVERYTHING SEASONING

1 tablespoon sesame seeds

1 tablespoon poppy seeds

1½ teaspoons dried garlic flakes

1 teaspoon dried minced onion

1 teaspoon kosher salt

## BISCUITS

2½ cups / 300 grams
    all-purpose flour, plus extra
    for folding and cutting

1 tablespoon baking powder

2 teaspoons kosher salt

1 tablespoon Everything
    Seasoning (recipe above)

1 cup plain full-fat kefir or
    buttermilk, cold

1 cup heavy cream, cold

## TOPPING

2 tablespoons full-fat
    buttermilk

2 tablespoons Everything
    Seasoning

If you like the garlicky, oniony goodness of everything bagels, you're going to love these biscuits, which also feature the naturally tangy flavor of kefir.

If you're unable to find kefir, buttermilk will work as a replacement. The combination of the fat in the kefir and heavy cream adds a creamy texture and light interior that makes these biscuits melt in your mouth. We're going to make our own everything seasoning, but feel free to use store-bought. These biscuits make a delicious breakfast sandwich with smoked salmon and cream cheese.

1. Adjust the oven rack to the middle position and preheat the oven to 450°F.

2. For the everything seasoning: Place the sesame seeds, poppy seeds, garlic flakes, minced onion, and salt in a small bowl and mix. Set aside.

3. For the biscuits: Place the flour, baking powder, salt, and everything seasoning in a large bowl and whisk to combine. Add the kefir and, using a spatula, gently fold it into the flour mixture, just to combine. Add the heavy cream and stir until the dough forms into a ball and no dry bits of flour are visible. The dough will be shaggy and sticky. If using buttermilk, you may need to add a few more tablespoons of flour, which should be added a tablespoon at a time.

4. Turn the dough onto a lightly floured surface and lightly dust with flour. With floured hands, pat the dough into a ½-inch-thick 11 × 6-inch rectangle. Fold the ends of the rectangle toward the center, one end on top of the other, to create a trifold. Dust the top lightly with flour, press out to the same size rectangle again, and repeat the folding. Repeat this process a third time. After the third folding, pat the dough to a ½-inch thickness and cut out the biscuits using a floured 3½-inch biscuit cutter. Be careful to press straight down and do not twist the cutter.

5. Place the biscuit rounds 1 inch apart on a parchment-lined baking sheet. Gather the scraps, reshape them, and pat the dough out to a ½-inch thickness. Cut out as above. Discard any remaining scraps.

6. For the topping: Brush the tops of the biscuits with the buttermilk and sprinkle with the everything seasoning.

7. Bake for 15 to 20 minutes, rotating the pan once halfway through, until the tops are golden brown. Serve immediately.

# Bacon Cheddar Biscuits

**YIELD: 6 TO 8 BISCUITS**

2½ cups / 300 grams
   all-purpose flour, plus extra
   for folding and cutting
1 tablespoon baking powder
2 teaspoons dried chives
1½ teaspoons freshly ground
   black pepper
1 teaspoon kosher salt
½ teaspoon baking soda
1 stick (8 tablespoons) unsalted
   butter, cold
1 cup finely diced crisp cooked
   bacon
1 cup shredded sharp cheddar
   cheese
1 cup full-fat buttermilk, cold

One of our most popular biscuits at the restaurant is studded with crisp bacon and cheddar cheese. It's used for a biscuit sandwich that's an elevated version of the classic bacon, egg, and cheese, so you get bacon and cheese in two forms (we'll make that sandwich later in this book). As these biscuits bake, the cheddar melts throughout each layer, creating pockets of gooey cheese that alternate with bits of bacon, a heavenly combination.

1. Adjust the oven rack to the middle position and preheat the oven to 450°F.

2. Place the flour, baking powder, dried chives, pepper, salt, and baking soda in a large bowl and whisk to combine.

3. Using the slicing side of a box grater, slice the butter into the flour mixture. Toss the sheets of butter in the flour. Add the bacon and cheddar and toss gently to combine. Then lightly work the butter pieces between your fingers or use a pastry cutter to break them up and coat them with flour. Stop when the dough resembles coarse sand and there are still some small visible pieces of butter.

4. Add the buttermilk and stir gently with a spatula until a dough forms into a ball and no dry bits of flour are visible. The dough will be shaggy and sticky.

5. Turn the dough onto a lightly floured surface and lightly dust with flour. With floured hands, pat the dough into a ½-inch-thick 11 × 6-inch rectangle. Fold the ends of the rectangle toward the center, one end on top of the other, to create a trifold. Dust the top lightly with flour, press out to the same size rectangle again, and repeat the folding. Repeat this process a third time. After the third folding, pat the dough to a ½-inch thickness and cut out the biscuits using a floured 2½-inch biscuit cutter. Be careful to press straight down and do not twist the cutter.

6. Place the biscuit rounds 1 inch apart on a parchment-lined baking sheet. Gather the scraps, reshape them, and pat the dough out to a ½-inch thickness. Cut out as above. Discard any remaining scraps.

7. Bake for 15 to 18 minutes, rotating the pan once halfway through, until the tops are golden brown. Serve immediately.

*Cook's Note: You can easily substitute cooked chicken or turkey sausage for the bacon.*

## Lift as you climb . . .

My maternal grandmother, Geraldine, was an educator who constantly stressed the importance of receiving a good education and also of seeing that all those around her did as well. In the 1940s, she played an integral part in opening a school in her small town of Goldsboro, North Carolina. Granny kept several books filled with photos of the East End Elementary School, where she taught, which I used to look through as a child. She would tell me the stories of all the children, the other teachers at the school, the neighborhood parades, and everything else in between. The lunchroom not only provided meals but was where home economics was taught. Children learned the basics of food preparation, including how dishes could be elevated by adding a little bit of this or a little of that. Long live the art of home economics!

Very early on in our venture, Jayla joined the team to run the front-of-house operations of our small biscuit business. She expressed an interest in learning the biscuit-baking process and quickly became my right hand in baking and running a growing business. I feel an immense sense of pride watching each pan of biscuits she pulls out of the oven. Wherever this journey of life takes her, she'll be one of the best biscuit bakers around.

# Sour Cream and Onion Biscuits

YIELD: 8 TO 10 BISCUITS

2 cups / 240 grams all-purpose
flour, plus extra for folding
and cutting

2 teaspoons baking powder

½ teaspoon kosher salt

1 cup chopped green onion,
white and green parts

1 cup sour cream, cold

3 tablespoons full-fat
buttermilk, cold

3 tablespoons salted butter,
melted (for brushing
the tops of the biscuits,
optional)

Sour cream biscuits have a delightful tang in each bite, and the addition of fresh green onions imparts a mild onion flavor. One of my weird sandwich combinations is crushed sour cream and onion potato chips and deviled ham. (Don't judge me; that's some good eating on a Sunday afternoon while bingeing Netflix.) Knowing that this flavor combo packed such a great punch, I thought, *Why not add a little bulk and make it into a powerhouse sandwich?* Whip up a batch of Deviled Ham (page 159) and enjoy them with me. If you're not into my TV snack style, these biscuits are great with pretty much anything, even a simple sandwich of a juicy slice of tomato sprinkled with black pepper and coarse salt.

1. Adjust the oven rack to the middle position and preheat the oven to 450°F.

2. Place the flour, baking powder, and salt in a large bowl and whisk to combine. Add the green onions and whisk until coated thoroughly.

3. Make a well in the center of the flour mixture and add the sour cream and buttermilk. Stir gently with a spatula until the dough begins to form into a ball and no dry bits of flour are visible. The dough will be shaggy and sticky.

4. Turn the dough onto a lightly floured surface and lightly dust with flour. With floured hands, pat the dough into a ½-inch-thick 11 × 6-inch rectangle. Fold the ends of the rectangle toward the center, one end on top of the other, to create a trifold. Dust the top lightly with flour, press out to the same size rectangle again, and repeat the folding. Repeat this process a third time. Pat the dough to a ½-inch thickness and cut out the biscuits using a floured 2½-inch biscuit cutter. Be careful to press straight down and do not twist the cutter.

5. Place the biscuits 1 inch apart on a parchment-lined baking sheet. Gather the scraps, reshape them, and pat the dough out to a ½-inch thickness. Cut out as above. Discard any remaining scraps.

6. Bake for 12 to 15 minutes, rotating the pan once halfway through, until golden brown. Brush the tops with melted butter (if using). Serve immediately.

# Flaky Ricotta Biscuits

YIELD: 8 BISCUITS

1½ cups / 180 grams all-purpose flour, plus extra for folding and cutting
2 teaspoons baking powder
1 teaspoon kosher salt
1 stick (8 tablespoons) unsalted butter, cold, cut into ½-inch pieces
1½ cups best-quality whole milk ricotta cheese, cold
1 large egg, beaten
2 tablespoons heavy cream, for brushing

Ricotta is a soft, creamy Italian cheese that is versatile and works in a litany of different baked goods. It's often featured in cakes and pancakes, and in this case, it adds a nice buttery flavor to biscuits. The egg also tenderizes the biscuits and increases the richness, and it works in tandem with the baking powder to give these a nice lift and flake. The dough will appear very shaggy when you mix in the ricotta and egg, but don't worry, it will all come together when you fold the dough out to shape the biscuits. I promise. If you're feeling fancy, add the zest of one lemon to the dough before rolling it out. Since these are light and airy, they'll go best with just a little Blackberry Jam (page 144) or honey.

1. Adjust the oven rack to the middle position and preheat the oven to 425°F.

2. Place the flour, baking powder, and salt in a large bowl and whisk to combine.

3. Add the butter and toss until well coated with the flour. Using your fingers or palms, flatten each piece of butter into a thin sheet. Toss the butter in the flour as you go to ensure each piece remains coated. When finished, each piece of butter should be about the size of a quarter.

4. Place the ricotta and egg in a small bowl and whisk to combine. Make a well in the center of the flour mixture and add the ricotta mixture. Using a spatula, stir gently until the dough begins to form into a ball and no dry bits of flour are visible. The dough will be shaggy and sticky.

5. Turn the dough onto a lightly floured surface and lightly dust with flour. With floured hands, pat the dough into a ½-inch-thick 11 × 6-inch rectangle. Fold the ends of the rectangle toward the center, one end on top of the other, to create a trifold. Dust the top lightly with flour, press out to the same size rectangle, and fold again. Repeat the process a third time. After the third folding, pat the dough to a ½-inch thickness. Use a sharp knife or bench scraper to cut 8 even-sized squares. Press straight down and do not use a sawing motion.

6. Place the biscuit squares 2 inches apart on a parchment-lined baking sheet. Brush the tops lightly with the heavy cream.

7. Bake for 16 to 18 minutes, rotating the pan once halfway through, until the tops are golden brown. Serve immediately.

# Sweet Potato Benne Seed Biscuits

**YIELD: 6 BISCUITS**

2 cups / 240 grams all-purpose flour, plus extra for folding and cutting

1 tablespoon baking powder

1 tablespoon sugar

1 teaspoon ground cinnamon

½ teaspoon kosher salt

¼ teaspoon baking soda

1 stick (8 tablespoons) unsalted butter, cold

1 cup mashed sweet potatoes, cold (about 1 medium potato)

¾ cup plus 2 tablespoons whole milk, cold

2 tablespoons benne seeds

2 tablespoons melted butter or honey, for brushing tops (optional)

*In late summer—the dog days, we called them—our work might be thinning the long vines off the sweet potatoes. We thinned out the vines because my father would say we'd only have little stringy potatoes if we didn't.*
—Mildred Edna Cotton Council

My paternal grandmother, Mildred Edna Cotton Council, founded Mama Dip's Kitchen restaurant in Chapel Hill, North Carolina, in 1976. The daughter of a sharecropper and granddaughter of an enslaved person, she built a culinary empire. Her sweet potato biscuits were one of her most popular dishes, and they are still featured on the menu today. Sweet potatoes add an earthy, sweet flavor to more than just your favorite pie. They make for a tender and moist biscuit that is great as a substitute for dinner rolls. These biscuits are the soul sisters of the basic buttermilk biscuits and are inspired by my grandmother's version. Make them whenever you have leftover sweet potatoes.

Benne seeds, an heirloom seed derived from the same plant as modern-day sesame seeds, were brought from West Africa by enslaved Africans who cultivated the seed and used the ingredient in many ways, such as to thicken stews, adding fat and protein to their food. Benne seeds add a rich and nutty flavor, and a brush of milk before baking will help to add color to the crust. I like to brush the baked biscuits with honey for extra sweetness, but you can opt for just butter or nothing at all.

1. Adjust the oven rack to the middle position and preheat the oven to 450°F.

2. Place the flour, baking powder, sugar, cinnamon, salt, and baking soda in a large bowl and whisk to combine.

3. Using the slicing side of a box grater, slice the butter into the flour mixture. Toss the sheets of butter in the flour until the butter is thoroughly coated. Then lightly work the butter pieces between your fingers or use a pastry cutter to break them up and coat them with flour. Stop when the dough resembles coarse sand and there are still some small visible pieces of butter.

4. Place the biscuit mixture into the freezer for 15 minutes.

5. Place the sweet potatoes and ¾ cup of the milk into a separate bowl and whisk to combine. Add the sweet potato mixture to the chilled flour mixture and stir gently with a spatula until the dough begins to form into a ball and no dry bits of flour are visible. The dough will be shaggy and sticky.

*Recipe continues*

6. Turn the dough onto a lightly floured surface and lightly dust with flour. With floured hands, gently pat the dough into a ½-inch-thick 11 × 6-inch rectangle. Fold the ends of the rectangle toward the center, one end on top of the other, to create a trifold. Dust the top lightly with flour, press out to the same size rectangle again, and repeat the folding. Repeat this process a third time. After the third folding, pat the dough to a ½-inch thickness and cut out the biscuits using a floured 3½-inch biscuit cutter. Be careful to press straight down and do not twist the cutter.

7. Place the biscuit rounds 1 inch apart on a parchment-lined baking sheet. Gather the scraps, reshape them, and pat them out to a ½-inch thickness. Cut out as above. Discard any remaining scraps.

8. Brush the tops of the biscuits with the remaining 2 tablespoons milk and sprinkle with the benne seeds.

9. Bake for 12 to 15 minutes, rotating the pan once halfway through, until the tops are golden brown. If desired, brush the tops of the baked biscuits with melted butter or honey. Serve immediately.

*Cook's Note: We are using a larger biscuit cutter for these biscuits because they'll be used later for sandwiches. If you opt for a smaller cutter, you'll yield more biscuits than noted.*

# Red Curry Basil Biscuits

**YIELD: 8 TO 10 BISCUITS**

2 cups / 240 grams all-purpose flour, plus extra for folding and cutting

2½ teaspoons baking powder

½ teaspoon kosher salt

6 tablespoons unsalted butter, cold

1 cup full-fat buttermilk, cold

2½ tablespoons Thai red curry paste

2 tablespoons finely chopped fresh basil

When it comes to new flavors for biscuits, nothing is truly off limits. I'm always looking for different ways to jazz up breakfast, and on any given day, you'll hear my husband say, "In a biscuit?!"

Red curry paste adds the flavor of ginger and garlic and a warm heat. These biscuits are great with fried chicken drizzled with cane syrup or simply spread with Hominy Honey Butter (page 150). You can also take the flavor up a notch by swapping out the buttermilk for coconut cream.

1. Adjust the oven rack to the middle position and preheat the oven to 450°F.

2. Place the flour, baking powder, and salt in a large bowl and whisk to combine.

3. Using the slicing side of a box grater, slice the butter into the flour mixture. Toss the sheets of butter in the flour to coat and evenly distribute. Then lightly work the butter pieces between your fingers or use a pastry cutter to break them up and coat them with flour. Stop when the dough resembles coarse sand and there are still some small visible pieces of butter.

4. Place the biscuit mixture into the freezer for 15 minutes.

5. Place the buttermilk, red curry paste, and chopped basil in a small bowl and whisk to combine. Add the buttermilk mixture to the flour mixture and stir gently with a spatula until the dough forms into a ball and no dry bits of flour are visible. The dough will be shaggy and sticky.

6. Turn the dough onto a lightly floured surface and lightly dust with flour. With floured hands, gently pat the dough into a ½-inch-thick 11 × 6-inch rectangle. Fold the ends of the rectangle toward the center, one end on top of the other, to create a trifold. Dust the top lightly with flour, press out to the same size rectangle again, and repeat the folding. Repeat this process a third time. After the third folding, pat the dough to a ½-inch thickness and cut out the biscuits using a floured 2½-inch biscuit cutter. Be careful to press straight down and do not twist the cutter.

7. Place the biscuit rounds 1 inch apart on a parchment-lined baking sheet. Gather the scraps, reshape them, and pat them out to a ½-inch thickness. Cut out as above. Discard any remaining scraps.

8. Bake for 12 to 15 minutes, rotating the pan once halfway through, until the tops are golden brown. Serve immediately.

## The First Lady of Tea Parties

The daughter of parents who were born into enslavement, Fannie Turner lived in her hometown of Goldsboro, North Carolina, for 103 years. Aunt Fannie's longevity made her a bottomless well of knowledge and wisdom. She had a regal, statuesque presence, despite her small frame. Each year as part of the church's annual Martha Washington tea party, she was given the honor of dressing as Martha, a role typically offered to the oldest parishioner. The tea party doubled as a church fundraiser, and attendees would come decked out in their floor-length gowns, fancy fox stoles, and white gloves. Finger foods were served on fine china with silver teapots and lacy tablecloths. Leafing through old images of these events, you see nothing but the finest of hats and brooches and, of course, food.

When researching older African American cookbooks, I found that they all had a recipe for tea biscuits, with a few detailing the tea parties the authors attended. In *Spoonbread & Strawberry Wine*, authors Norma Jean and Carole Darden share the story of Aunt Artelia and her knack for innovative cooking, with her specialty being breads. They include a recipe for tea biscuits that calls for using cake yeast, potatoes, and eggs.

My Aunt Fannie (top left) dressed as Martha Washington, and
other elegantly dressed tea party guests. The year is 1970.

# Afternoon Tea Biscuits with Honey Bourbon Butter

**YIELD: 15 OR 16 BISCUITS**

## BISCUITS

2 cups / 240 grams all-purpose flour, plus extra for folding and cutting

1 tablespoon baking powder

1 teaspoon kosher salt

¼ cup vegetable shortening, cold, broken into small pieces

1 cup mashed potatoes, cold

3 tablespoons finely chopped fresh tarragon

7 tablespoons full-fat buttermilk, cold

## HONEY BOURBON BUTTER

1 stick (8 tablespoons) unsalted butter, room temperature

¼ cup honey

2 tablespoons bourbon

This recipe for tea biscuits skips the cake yeast and eggs but does include potatoes, giving the biscuits the lightest texture. (This is a great use for leftover mashed potatoes.) Tarragon adds a bitter, sweet, and almost peppery taste, with notes of mint and vanilla.

1. Adjust the oven rack to the middle position and preheat the oven to 450°F.

2. For the biscuits: Place the flour, baking powder, and salt in a large bowl and whisk to combine.

3. Using your fingers, a pastry cutter, or a fork, work the shortening into the flour mixture until only pea-sized pieces of shortening remain. Add the mashed potatoes and use your fingers or the pastry cutter to incorporate until the mixture resembles coarse "feta-like" crumbles. Refrigerate for 10 minutes.

4. Add the tarragon and buttermilk and use a spatula to stir until the dough forms into a ball and no dry bits of flour are visible. The dough will be shaggy and sticky.

5. Turn the dough onto a lightly floured surface and lightly dust with flour. With floured hands or a rolling pin, pat or roll the dough to a ½-inch-thick 11 × 6-inch rectangle. Fold the ends of the rectangle toward the center, one end on top of the other, to create a trifold. Dust the top lightly with flour, press or roll out to the same size rectangle again, and repeat the folding. Repeat this process a third time. After the third folding, pat or roll the dough to a ½-inch thickness and cut out the biscuits using a floured 2-inch biscuit cutter. Be careful to press straight down and do not twist the cutter.

6. Place the biscuit rounds 1 inch apart on a parchment-lined baking sheet. Gather the scraps, reshape them, and pat the dough out to a ½-inch thickness. Cut out as above. Discard any remaining scraps.

7. Bake for 12 to 13 minutes, rotating the pan once halfway through, until the tops are golden brown.

8. While the biscuits are baking, make the honey bourbon butter: Place the butter, honey, and bourbon in a medium bowl and whisk until smooth, 2 to 3 minutes.

9. Remove the biscuits from the oven, generously brush the tops of each biscuit with the honey bourbon butter, and serve immediately. Use any leftover butter to spread on the biscuits once split.

*Cook's Note: Since these biscuits are fit for tea, the recipe calls for a 2-inch biscuit cutter, which will give you bite-sized biscuits. You can, of course, use a larger cutter, but please note that the yield will be less.*

# Corn Milk Biscuits

YIELD: 14 OR 15 BISCUITS

### CORN MILK

2 ears fresh corn, kernels
  removed from the cob
½ cup full-fat buttermilk, cold
1 tablespoon sugar

### BISCUITS

3 cups / 360 grams all-purpose
  flour, plus extra for folding
  and cutting
1 tablespoon baking powder
1 teaspoon kosher salt
1 stick (8 tablespoons)
  unsalted butter, cold, plus
  2 tablespoons, melted
½ cup full-fat buttermilk, cold

In my early twenties, I moved to South Carolina, not knowing anyone besides my partner and his family at the time. Moving to a small town to follow a man was a terrible idea, but that's not what this book is about, so let me get on with it. I met a young lady around my age where I was working. She took me under her wing and became a source of comfort in a strange place. She was "from down there," so her family all lived close by. Visiting her aunt once, I watched as they cut cobs of corn and mashed the kernels in a pot. My friend said her aunt was making corn pudding bread, which was similar to spoon bread. After baking, it was absolutely spectacular. The "bread" was crisp on the top and bottom, but the interior had a gooey corn custard consistency that was extremely sweet. Almost twenty years later, I've yet to taste anything quite like it. In the spirit of my friend's aunt and the recipe she would never share, I started making a sweet creamed-corn base for biscuits. Using fresh corn with a little sugar and buttermilk makes these biscuits buttery with a bit of tang and sweetness.

These biscuits pair nicely with Blueberry Lemon Jam (page 147) or Blackberry Jam (page 144). A tablespoon of fresh herbs, such as mint, parsley, or basil, can also be used to jazz these biscuits up.

1. Adjust the oven rack to the middle position and preheat the oven to 450°F.

2. For the corn milk: Place the corn kernels, buttermilk, and sugar into the bowl of a food processor and pulse until only small pieces of corn are still visible, 10 to 12 pulses. Set aside.

3. For the biscuits: Place the flour, baking powder, and salt in a large bowl and whisk to combine.

4. Using the slicing side of a box grater, slice the butter into the flour mixture. Toss the sheets of butter in the flour to completely coat the butter and evenly distribute it. Then lightly work the butter pieces between your fingers or use a pastry cutter to break them up and coat them with flour. Stop when the dough resembles coarse sand and there are still some small visible pieces of butter.

5. Add the corn milk and buttermilk and stir gently with a spatula until the dough begins to form into a ball and no dry bits of flour are visible. The dough will be shaggy and sticky.

*Recipe continues*

6. Turn the dough onto a lightly floured surface and lightly dust with flour. With floured hands, pat the dough into a ½-inch-thick 11 × 6-inch rectangle. Fold the ends of the rectangle toward the center, one end on top of the other, to create a trifold. Dust the top lightly with flour, press out to the same size rectangle again, and repeat the folding. Repeat this process a third time. After the third folding, pat the dough to a ½-inch thickness and cut out the biscuits using a floured 2½-inch biscuit cutter. Be careful to press straight down and do not twist the cutter.

7. Place the biscuits ½ inch apart on a baking sheet. Gather the scraps, reshape them, and pat the dough out to a ½-inch thickness. Cut out as above. Discard any remaining scraps.

8. Bake for 15 to 17 minutes, rotating the pan once halfway through, until the tops are golden brown. Brush the tops with the melted butter. Serve immediately.

# Chive and Red Pepper Cornmeal Biscuits

YIELD: 8 BISCUITS

2 cups / 240 grams all-purpose flour, plus extra for folding and cutting

1 cup / 156 grams yellow cornmeal

1 tablespoon baking powder

1 teaspoon kosher salt

½ teaspoon baking soda

1 stick (8 tablespoons) unsalted butter, cold

1¼ cups full-fat buttermilk, cold

3 tablespoons dried chives

2 tablespoons red pepper flakes

2 tablespoons salted butter, melted

This is the perfect biscuit to serve alongside a bowl of chili or soup. The cornmeal and spices, along with hints of fire from the red pepper flakes, give them a bit of an attitude.

1. Adjust the oven rack to the middle position and preheat the oven to 450°F.

2. Place the flour, cornmeal, baking powder, salt, and baking soda in a large bowl and whisk to combine.

3. Using the slicing side of a box grater, slice the butter into the flour mixture. Toss the sheets of butter in the flour. Then lightly work the butter pieces between your fingers or use a pastry cutter to break them up and coat them with flour. Stop when the dough resembles coarse sand and there are still some small visible pieces of butter.

4. Add the buttermilk, chives, and red pepper flakes and stir gently with a spatula until the dough forms into a ball and no dry bits of flour are visible. The dough will be sticky and shaggy.

5. Turn the dough onto a lightly floured surface and lightly dust with flour. With floured hands, pat the dough into a ½-inch-thick 11 × 6-inch rectangle. Fold the ends of the rectangle toward the center, one end on top of the other, to create a trifold. Dust the top lightly with flour, press into the same size rectangle again, and repeat the folding. Repeat this process a third time. After the third folding, pat the dough to a ½-inch thickness and cut out the biscuits using a floured 3½-inch biscuit cutter. Be careful to press straight down and do not twist the cutter.

6. Place the biscuit rounds on a parchment-lined baking sheet or in a cast-iron skillet. For fluffy, pull-apart biscuits, place the biscuits close together. For crispy edges, space 1 inch apart. Gather the scraps, reshape them, and pat the dough out to a ½-inch thickness. Cut out as above. Discard any remaining scraps.

7. Bake for 16 to 18 minutes, rotating the pan once halfway through, until the tops are golden brown. Brush the tops with the melted butter. Serve immediately.

# Cornmeal Cream Biscuits

**YIELD: 8 TO 10 BISCUITS**

1 cup / 120 grams self-rising flour, plus extra for folding and cutting

1 cup / 122 grams stone-ground yellow cornmeal

2 tablespoons sugar

1¼ cups heavy cream, cold

Self-rising flour can be tricky to locate in certain areas. Here's a quick recipe to whip up your own.

**SELF-RISING FLOUR**

1 cup all-purpose flour

1½ teaspoons baking powder

½ teaspoon kosher salt

Whisk together the flour, baking powder, and salt.

While biscuits play a starring role in the cast of quick breads, cornbread is truly my favorite quick bread to eat. Here are cornbread-inspired biscuits that combine the two quick breads with a bit of sugar. The cornmeal makes the biscuit more crumbly and less flaky and gives it good corn flavor. And in the spirit of "quick" breads, this recipe cuts corners so these biscuits come together fast. Heavy cream is both the fat and the liquid, and self-rising flour gives us the fluffy rise that we love so much.

These biscuits are wonderful with a smear or two of Tomato Jam (page 148), combining the best of summer produce.

1. Adjust the oven rack to the middle position and preheat the oven to 450°F.

2. Place the flour, cornmeal, and sugar in a large bowl and whisk to combine.

3. Make a well in the center and add the cream. Stir gently with a spatula until the dough forms into a ball and there are no dry bits of flour visible. The dough will be shaggy and sticky.

4. Turn the dough onto a lightly floured surface and lightly dust with flour. With floured hands, pat the dough into a ½-inch-thick 11 × 6-inch rectangle. Fold the ends of the rectangle toward the center, one on top of the other, to create a trifold. Dust the top lightly with flour, press out to the same size rectangle again, and repeat the folding. Repeat this process a third time. After the third folding, pat the dough to a ½-inch thickness and cut out the biscuits using a floured 2½-inch biscuit cutter. Be careful to press straight down and do not twist the cutter.

5. Place the biscuit rounds 1 inch apart on a parchment-lined baking sheet or in a cast-iron skillet. Gather the scraps, reshape them, and pat the dough out to a ½-inch thickness. Cut out as above. Discard any remaining scraps.

6. Bake for 10 to 15 minutes, rotating the pan once halfway through, until the tops are golden brown. Serve immediately.

# Jalapeño Cheddar Biscuits

YIELD: 6 BISCUITS

2½ cups / 300 grams
   all-purpose flour, plus extra
   for folding and cutting
1 tablespoon baking powder
1 teaspoon kosher salt
½ teaspoon baking soda
1 stick (8 tablespoons) unsalted
   butter, cold
1 cup (about 4 ounces)
   shredded sharp cheddar
   cheese
4-ounce can diced jalapeños,
   drained
1¼ cups full-fat buttermilk, cold

BYOB, or build-your-own biscuit, is one of the most popular options at my restaurant. Some customers just add bacon, while some will add sausage, eggs, bacon, fried chicken, *and* gravy all to one sandwich—true story. But our manager, Jayla, can preach the gospel of the best combinations like the true biscuit evangelist she has become. This jalapeño cheddar biscuit has been used in every combination you can imagine, but nothing beats it with our hot honey fried chicken. I'm a little basic, so I prefer just an over easy egg running down the crispy biscuit edges.

Since fresh jalapeños can vary so much in flavor and heat, using canned jalapeños actually helps to make sure the flavors are as close as possible to what I serve. Also, canned jalapeños come with a little pickled essence that really enhances the flavor of these biscuits.

1. Adjust the oven rack to the middle position and preheat the oven to 450°F.

2. Place the flour, baking powder, salt, and baking soda in a large bowl and whisk to combine.

3. Using the slicing side of a box grater, slice the butter into the flour mixture. Toss the sheets of butter in the flour. Add the cheddar and jalapeños and toss gently to combine. Then lightly work the butter pieces between your fingers or use a pastry cutter to break them up and coat them with flour. Stop when the dough resembles coarse sand and there are still some small visible pieces of butter.

4. Add the buttermilk and stir gently with a spatula until the dough forms into a ball and no dry bits of flour are visible. The dough will be shaggy and sticky.

5. Turn the dough onto a lightly floured surface and lightly dust with flour. With floured hands, pat the dough into a ½-inch-thick 11 × 6-inch rectangle. Fold the ends of the rectangle toward the center, one end on top of the other, to create a trifold. Dust the top lightly with flour, press out to the same size rectangle again, and repeat the folding. Repeat this process a third time. After the third folding, pat the dough to a ½-inch thickness and cut out the biscuits using a floured 3½-inch biscuit cutter. Be careful to press straight down and do not twist the cutter.

6. Place the biscuit rounds 1 inch apart on a parchment-lined baking sheet. Gather the scraps, reshape them, and pat the dough out to a ½-inch thickness. Cut out as above. Discard any remaining scraps.

7. Bake for 15 to 18 minutes, rotating the pan once halfway through, until the tops are golden brown. Serve immediately.

# 6.
# SWEET BISCUITS

# Deep-Fried Drop Biscuits with Cinnamon Sugar

YIELD: 10 OR 11 BISCUITS

## CINNAMON SUGAR

½ cup sugar
1 teaspoon ground cinnamon

## BISCUITS

2 cups / 240 grams all-purpose
    flour, plus extra for folding
    and cutting
2 teaspoons baking powder
2 tablespoons sugar
¾ teaspoon kosher salt
½ teaspoon baking soda
1¼ cups full-fat buttermilk, cold
1 stick (8 tablespoons) unsalted
    butter, melted
Peanut or other neutral oil, for
    frying

These biscuits taste like old-fashioned doughnuts. This recipe utilizes the drop biscuit method, but instead of baking the biscuits, we fry them in bubbling hot grease, which creates a crisp exterior that surrounds the soft biscuit crumb we love. In the summer, we serve a limited supply of these at Bomb Biscuit Co., fresh out of the fryer—rolled in cinnamon sugar with a side of Georgia Peach Mango Jam (page 145) to dunk each biscuit in before devouring. Be sure to have some napkins on hand; these can get a little messy.

1. For the cinnamon sugar: Place the sugar and cinnamon in a medium bowl and whisk to combine. Set aside.

2. For the biscuits: Place the flour, baking powder, sugar, salt, and baking soda in a large bowl and whisk to combine.

3. Place the buttermilk and warm melted butter in a small bowl and stir until the butter forms small clumps and the mixture looks curdled (you should see bits of butter throughout). Add the buttermilk mixture to the flour mixture and stir gently with a spatula until the ingredients are incorporated and the mixture pulls away slightly from the edges of the bowl. The dough will be shaggy and sticky.

4. In a 6-quart heavy-bottomed pot or Dutch oven over medium-high heat, heat 1 to 1½ inches of peanut oil to 375°F.

5. Using a greased ¼-cup measure, carefully scoop the dough, 3 or 4 at a time, into the oil and fry until golden brown and cooked through, 4 to 5 minutes, flipping halfway through. Using a slotted spoon, transfer the biscuits to the cooling rack to drain for 10 to 15 seconds.

6. Transfer the biscuits to the bowl with the cinnamon sugar mixture and toss to coat. (You can also put the cinnamon sugar in a medium paper bag and shake to coat.) Place the coated biscuits back on the rack to cool for about 5 minutes before serving. Repeat with the remaining dough. Serve immediately.

# For the Love of Big Mama and Biscuits

Sara Strickland Gavin was my maternal great-grandmother. I would be a teenager before I knew what her actual name was, as Big Mama was how she was always referred to, even by those in the community of no kin to us. She was an enigma of sorts; there are no records of her birth, just a story of how she was born on Phelps Alley, which no longer exists in our small town of Goldsboro. There are stories of her ability to "pass," which allowed her to be sent to the whites-only grocery store unnoticed as a young girl, and endless recountings of the resolute woman who baked the best biscuits, sweet potato pie, and crushed pineapple cake, according to everyone. And she kept a pistol in a box by her foot during the riots of '68, according to my mother.

She left a notecard of her recipe for sweet potato pie for her daughter decades before I was born, and I've made it now more times than I can count. I've also baked biscuits on a slightly rusted sheet pan that once belonged to her and learned how to crimp pie edges she'd approve of. As children, many dream of becoming doctors, lawyers, astronauts. I just wanted to be a Big Mama: an omnipresent figure that would be remembered forever for her biscuits, coconut cake, and Colt .45 pistol.

The recipes in this chapter are mostly inspired by Black culinary icons, but I dedicate the chapter to my great-grandmother, Sara Gavin, who mastered the art of both biscuits and sweets.

# Apple Butter Drop Biscuits

**YIELD: 10 TO 12 BISCUITS**

1¼ cups / 150 grams all-purpose flour, plus extra for folding and cutting

¾ cup / 84 grams whole wheat flour

2 teaspoons sugar

¾ teaspoon kosher salt

½ teaspoon baking soda

1 stick (8 tablespoons) unsalted butter, cold, cut into cubes

½ cup full-fat buttermilk, cold

½ cup Valerie's Apple Butter (page 152)

When I was in college, there was a lady who sold baked goods not too far from campus. She had all kinds of breads and muffins, giving the college kids a special discount. My favorite was a dark brown, heavily spiced loaf that was made with apple butter and topped with a drizzle of some molasses-based confection. I could eat the whole thing before making it to class. This is my homage to that bread and the wonderful woman who made it.

Apple butter is essentially apples cooked down and caramelized in sugar. Adding some to the dough gives the biscuits an intense flavor of apples, and with hints of warm cinnamon spice, they taste like fall. These drop biscuits are delicious by themselves; however, a smear of ricotta cheese with a sprinkle of lemon zest adds some pizzazz. For a savory option, slice a biscuit in half and grate a little cheddar over each slice, place it in the oven just long enough for the cheese to melt, and you've got yourself one major grilled cheese biscuit.

1. Adjust the oven rack to the middle position and preheat the oven to 450°F.

2. Place the all-purpose flour, whole wheat flour, sugar, salt, and baking soda in a large bowl and whisk to combine. Scatter the butter over the surface of the flour and lightly work the butter pieces between your fingers or use a pastry cutter to break them up and coat them with flour. Stop when the dough resembles coarse sand and there are still some small visible pieces of butter.

3. Make a well in the center of the mixture and add the buttermilk. Stir with a spatula just until the dough comes together. Add the apple butter and continue to stir until the ingredients are incorporated and the mixture pulls away slightly from the edges of the bowl. The dough will be shaggy and sticky.

4. Using a ¼-cup measuring cup or scoop, drop the dough onto a parchment-lined baking sheet, 1 inch apart. If you want smaller or larger biscuits, adjust the portion size as desired.

5. Bake for 15 to 20 minutes, rotating the pan once halfway through, until the tops are golden brown. Serve immediately.

# Honey Roasted Peach Biscuits

**YIELD: 12 TO 14 BISCUITS**

8 peaches (about 2 pounds), peeled and chopped

1½ teaspoons freshly squeezed lemon juice

3 tablespoons honey

2 tablespoons light brown sugar

½ teaspoon ground cardamom

3 cups / 455 grams self-rising flour (see pages 18 and 114), plus extra for folding and cutting

2¼ cups plus 1 tablespoon heavy cream, cold

1 large egg

2 to 3 tablespoons turbinado sugar

Irene Jackson, or Aunt Rene, as I called her, was an alluring figure. She wore turbans and brooches that dazzled in the sunlight and had a pet Chihuahua that sat on her shoulder as she drove down the streets of Goldsboro in her Cutlass. Aunt Rene and my granny were dear friends who shared the week's gossip on the way to church every Sunday, and I rode in the back pretending not to listen to grown folks' conversation. Aunt Rene could make desserts that would rival my granny's, although I'd never say as much, one being the most delightful shortcakes that tasted like a combination of a biscuit and cake filled with some type of fruit and topped with whipped cream. While hers were sliced like a cake, they still had the texture of a creamy biscuit.

Here I've invoked the spirit of my Aunt Rene's fruit-filled shortcake with a basic cream biscuit folded over roasted peaches flavored with honey and a little bit of cardamom.

This is one of the simplest ways to make biscuits from scratch; you can skip the peaches and use any fruit to transform it into an incredible variety of shortcake-style biscuits. Add a dollop of whipped cream if you're feeling fancy.

1. Adjust the oven rack to the middle position and preheat the oven to 350°F.

2. Place the peaches in a large bowl and toss well with the lemon juice. Add the honey, brown sugar, and cardamom and toss to combine. Transfer the peach mixture to a parchment-lined baking sheet and roast until the peaches are tender, 25 to 30 minutes, turning them over halfway through roasting. Let cool completely.

3. Increase the oven temperature to 450°F.

4. Place the flour in a large bowl and make a well in the center. Add 2¼ cups of the heavy cream and stir gently with a spatula until the dough forms into a ball and no dry bits of flour are visible. The dough will be shaggy and sticky.

5. Turn the dough onto a lightly floured surface and lightly dust with flour. With floured hands, pat the dough into a ½-inch-thick 11 × 6-inch rectangle. Fold the ends of the rectangle toward the center, one end on top of the other, to create a trifold. Dust the top lightly with flour and pat out again to a ¼-inch-thick, 20- to 22-inch-long rectangle.

6. Using a slotted spoon, spoon the cooled peaches over half the length of the rectangle. Fold the other half of the dough over the top of the peaches. Pinch all around to seal the peaches in the dough. Using a knife or bench scraper, cut straight down to create 12 to 14 biscuits. Gently place the biscuits 1 inch apart on a parchment-lined baking sheet.

7. Whisk the egg and the remaining tablespoon of heavy cream in a small bowl. Gently brush the tops of each biscuit with the egg wash. Sprinkle the tops with the turbinado sugar.

8. Bake for 12 to 15 minutes, rotating the pan halfway through, until the tops are golden brown. Serve warm.

# Blueberry Lemon Dumplings

YIELD: 4 TO 6 SERVINGS

### DUMPLINGS

2 cups / 240 grams all-purpose
  flour, plus extra for folding
  and shaping
2 teaspoons baking soda
1 teaspoon sugar
¾ teaspoon kosher salt
Zest of 1 lemon
1 stick (8 tablespoons) unsalted
  butter, cold, cut into ½-inch
  pieces
¾ cup full-fat buttermilk, cold

### BLUEBERRY SAUCE

1 pound (about 3 cups) fresh
  blueberries
1 cup sugar

In Sallie Ann Robinson's cookbook *Gullah Home Cooking the Daufuskie Way*, she tells stories of growing up on Daufuskie Island in South Carolina. In the book she shares a recipe for roadside blueberry biscuits that her grandmother made.

Instead of tossing the blueberries into the biscuit dough, I decided to turn things around here and drop biscuit dough into bubbling blueberry sauce. A bit of lemon zest added to the dough intensifies the flavor of the dumplings. This dish is best served warm and eaten with a spoon—and maybe a scoop of ice cream.

1. For the dumplings: Place the flour, baking soda, sugar, and salt in a large bowl and whisk to combine. Add the lemon zest and whisk again. Lightly work the butter pieces into the flour mixture with your fingers or a pastry cutter until the dough resembles coarse sand and there are still some small visible pieces of butter.

2. Add the buttermilk and stir gently with a spatula until a soft dough forms. Place the bowl in the fridge while you make the blueberry sauce.

3. For the blueberry sauce: In a 4- to 6-quart saucepan over medium-high heat, combine the blueberries, sugar, and 2 cups of water and bring the mixture to a boil, stirring frequently, about 7 minutes.

4. Take the dough out of the refrigerator and, using a 2-tablespoon ice cream scoop, carefully scoop the dough into the boiling blueberry sauce. Once all the dumplings have been added, reduce the heat to low to maintain a simmer, cover, and cook until the dumplings are cooked through (the center should be fluffy and not doughy), 18 to 20 minutes. Do not stir the dumplings while they cook.

5. Serve the dumplings warm, with a little extra blueberry sauce over the top.

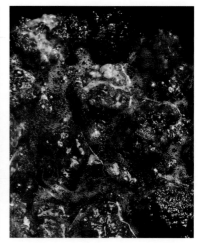

# Rosemary Orange Cream Biscuits

**YIELD: 9 OR 10 BISCUITS**

2½ cups / 300 grams all-purpose flour, plus extra for folding and cutting
1 tablespoon baking powder
1 tablespoon sugar
1 teaspoon kosher salt
1 cup heavy cream, cold
Zest of 1 orange
¼ cup freshly squeezed orange juice
3 tablespoons finely chopped fresh rosemary

Lena Richard was a pioneer of food TV, achieving great acclaim during the Jim Crow era in the South. In 1949 and 1950, her cooking show aired every Tuesday and Thursday on WDSU, where you could catch her teaching you how to cook your way through her *New Orleans Cookbook*, which was published in 1940.

Born in 1892, Lena's culinary career began when she was a domestic worker alongside her mother. It was in this role that her culinary skills radiated brightly, and she attended the renowned Fannie Farmer Cooking School in Boston. Upon graduation, she returned to New Orleans and created a catering business, opened a lunch house, wrote a cookbook, and went on to receive national recognition as head chef of the Travis House in Colonial Williamsburg.

As a gift several years ago, my husband gave me an original copy of her book. One of my favorite recipes is her orange biscuits, which call for dipping sugar cubes in orange juice and placing them on top of the biscuits before baking. Drawing inspiration from this recipe, I add orange juice, zest, and rosemary to a tender cream biscuit. The balance of sweet and tart varies depending on the type of orange used. Rosemary is an aromatic herb that has lemony pine notes, intensifying the flavor of this biscuit.

1. Adjust the oven rack to the middle position and preheat the oven to 400°F.

2. Place the flour, baking powder, sugar, and salt in a large bowl and whisk to combine.

3. Make a well in the center of the flour mixture and add the cream. Stir gently with a spatula until the ingredients are incorporated. Add the orange zest, orange juice, and rosemary and stir until the dough forms into a ball and no dry bits of flour are visible. The dough will be shaggy and sticky.

4. Turn the dough onto a lightly floured surface and lightly dust with flour. With floured hands or a rolling pin, pat or roll the dough into a ½-inch-thick 11 × 6-inch rectangle. Fold the ends of the rectangle toward the center, one end on top of the other, to create a trifold. Dust the top lightly with flour, press or roll out to the same size rectangle again, and repeat the folding. Repeat the process a third time. After the third folding, pat or roll the dough to a ½-inch thickness and cut out the biscuits using a floured 2½-inch biscuit cutter. Be careful to press straight down and do not twist the cutter.

5. Place the biscuit rounds 1 inch apart on a parchment-lined baking sheet. Gather the scraps, reshape them, and pat the dough out to a ½-inch thickness. Cut out as above. Discard any remaining scraps.

6. Bake for 10 to 15 minutes, rotating the pan once halfway through, until the tops are golden brown. Serve immediately.

*Still We Rise*

# Hawaiian Sweet Biscuits

YIELD: 12 TO 15 BISCUITS

## BISCUITS

¾ cup canned pineapple juice, cold

5 tablespoons light brown sugar

½ ounce active dry yeast

5 cups / 600 grams all-purpose flour, plus extra for folding and cutting

2 teaspoons baking powder

1½ teaspoons kosher salt

1 teaspoon baking soda

½ cup vegetable shortening, cold, broken into pea-sized pieces

1 stick (8 tablespoons) unsalted butter, cold

1½ cups full-fat buttermilk, cold

## MAPLE BUTTER

3 tablespoons salted butter, melted

2 tablespoons maple syrup

There is no shame in buying store-bought bread when the occasion calls for it. When it comes to those King's Hawaiian Sweet Rolls, that occasion is at least once a week for me. They are soft, squishy, just a little sweet, addictive, and a common fixture at every Sunday dinner, cookout, and church fish fry I've attended in the past few years. My mother refers to them as "the rolls," and you're just supposed to know what they are and have them ready when it's time to set the table.

Because of my slight obsession with biscuits, my mind immediately went to how these rolls could come to life in the form of a biscuit. The addition of pineapple juice and brown sugar to my super-light, yeasted "angel"-style biscuits got me there. Then I add a slathering of maple butter on the tops for a little extra sweetness.

At Bomb Biscuit Co., we make a few special sandwiches using this biscuit—from our habanero peach fried chicken to our country ham and muenster cheese. The light sweetness makes them perfect for any sweet-and-savory (especially sweet-savory-and-spicy) combination.

1. Adjust the oven rack to the middle position and preheat the oven to 450°F.

2. For the biscuits: In a small saucepan, heat ¼ cup of the pineapple juice to 110°F. Place the warm pineapple juice, 2 tablespoons of the brown sugar, and the yeast in a small bowl and gently stir to combine. Set aside until bubbles form on the surface of the mixture, 3 to 4 minutes.

3. Place the remaining 3 tablespoons brown sugar, flour, baking powder, salt, and baking soda in a large bowl and whisk to combine. Using your fingers, a pastry cutter, or a fork, work the shortening into the flour mixture until only pea-sized pieces of shortening remain. Using the slicing side of a box grater, slice the butter into the flour mixture. Toss the sheets of butter in the flour and then lightly work the butter pieces between your fingers or use a pastry cutter to break them up and coat them with flour. Stop when the dough resembles coarse sand and there are still some small visible pieces of butter.

4. Make a well in the center of the mixture and add the yeast mixture, buttermilk, and remaining ½ cup pineapple juice. Stir gently with a spatula until the dough forms into a ball and no dry bits of flour are visible. The dough will be shaggy and sticky. Cover the bowl with plastic wrap and set aside to rest at room temperature for 1 hour. The dough may rise slightly.

*Recipe continues*

5. Turn the dough onto a lightly floured surface and lightly dust with flour. With floured hands, pat the dough into a ½-inch-thick 11 × 6-inch rectangle. Fold the ends of the rectangle toward the center, one end on top of the other, to create a trifold. Dust lightly with flour, press out to the same size rectangle again, and repeat the folding. Repeat this process a third time. After the third folding, pat the dough to a ½-inch thickness and cut out the biscuits using a floured 3½-inch biscuit cutter. Be careful to press straight down and do not twist the cutter.

6. Place the biscuit rounds 1 inch apart on a parchment-lined baking sheet. Gather the scraps, reshape them, and pat them out to a ½-inch thickness. Cut out the biscuits as above. Discard any remaining scraps.

7. Bake for 15 to 20 minutes, rotating the pan once halfway through, until the tops are golden brown.

8. While the biscuits are baking, make the maple butter: Place the melted butter and maple syrup in a small bowl and whisk to combine.

9. Remove the biscuits from the oven and brush with the maple butter. Serve immediately.

# Chocolate Chip Biscuits

**YIELD: 12 OR 13 BISCUITS**

2½ cups / 300 grams all-
purpose flour, plus extra for
folding and cutting
1 tablespoon baking powder
1½ teaspoons kosher salt
½ teaspoon baking soda
2 tablespoons vegetable
shortening, cold, cut into
½-inch chunks
1 stick (8 tablespoons) unsalted
butter, cold
1½ cups full-fat buttermilk, cold
½ cup (4 ounces) semisweet
chocolate chips

If there is a way to incorporate chocolate into any dish, I'm going to find it. These biscuits are studded with chocolate chips that melt into the layers of the dough as it bakes. They've become somewhat of a signature item at Bomb Biscuit Co., where we often end up selling them by the dozen rather than just ones or twos. We're that happy place where biscuit lovers and chocolate enthusiasts meet. Each bite is like eating a biscuit that's been dipped in chocolate gravy, which I highly recommend. The recipe calls for semisweet chocolate chips, but you can switch things up and use dark chocolate, too.

1. Adjust the oven rack to the middle position and preheat the oven to 450°F.

2. Place the flour, baking powder, salt, and baking soda in a large bowl and whisk to combine.

3. Using your fingers, a pastry cutter, or a fork, work the shortening into the flour mixture until only pea-sized pieces of shortening remain. Using the slicing side of a box grater, slice the butter into the flour mixture. Toss the sheets of butter in the flour. Then lightly work the butter pieces between your fingers or use a pastry cutter to break them up and coat them with flour. Stop when the dough resembles coarse sand and there are still some small visible pieces of butter.

4. Place the biscuit mixture into the freezer for 15 minutes.

5. Add the buttermilk and stir gently with a spatula until the dough forms into a ball and no dry bits of flour are visible. The dough will be shaggy and sticky.

6. Turn the dough onto a lightly floured surface and lightly dust with flour. With floured hands, pat the dough into a ½-inch-thick 11 × 6-inch rectangle. Fold the ends of the rectangle toward the center, one end on top of the other, to create a trifold. Sprinkle the chocolate chips evenly over the dough. Using your hands or a rolling pin, press the chips into the dough. Dust the top lightly with flour, press out to the same size rectangle again, and repeat the folding and sprinkling of chocolate chips. Repeat this process a third time. After the third folding, pat the dough to a ½-inch thickness and cut out the biscuits using a floured 2½-inch biscuit cutter. Be careful to press straight down and do not twist the cutter.

7. Place the biscuit rounds 1 inch apart on a parchment-lined baking sheet. Gather the scraps, reshape them, and pat the dough out to a ½-inch thickness. Cut out as above. Discard any remaining scraps.

8. Bake for 15 to 17 minutes, rotating the pan once halfway through, until the tops are golden brown. Serve immediately.

*Still We Rise*

# The Disappearance of a Princess

*A lot of them smart sayin's ain't so smart. Like if at first you don't succeed.*
*Many's the time in this world, your batter goes in that oven once.*

—Princess Pamela

Several years ago, the story of the illustrious Princess Pamela was given mainstream life when her cookbook, originally published in 1969, was reissued. I'd acquired an original copy of *Princess Pamela's Soul Food Cookbook* many years prior, not knowing much about the author or the Little Kitchen, a restaurant Pamela ran out of her small Manhattan apartment.

   Pamela Strobel, which may not have been her real name, was born in Spartanburg, South Carolina, but after the death of her mother and grandmother, she moved to New York. Seeming to reinvent herself, Pamela became an iconic culinary figure who hosted many patrons from all walks of life in her establishment. But after years of adulation, she has not been seen or heard from since 1998, a mystery that has not been solved.[*]

   (My mother often asks if her whereabouts have been discovered.)

---

[*] Black women and girls go missing at alarming rates. In 2020, of the 268,000+ girls and women reported missing, nearly 34% of them were Black, even though Black women and girls account for less than 15% of the United States population. Currently there are nearly 100,000 black women and girls missing in the US.

—Data from the Black and Missing Foundation, Inc., a nonprofit organization whose mission is to bring awareness to missing persons of color

# Peanut Butter and Cane Syrup Biscuits

**YIELD: 8 TO 10 BISCUITS**

2½ cups / 300 grams
    all-purpose flour, plus extra
    for folding and cutting

2 tablespoons light brown
    sugar

1 tablespoon baking powder

1 teaspoon kosher salt

½ teaspoon baking soda

¼ teaspoon ground cinnamon

3 tablespoons cane syrup;
    honey or maple syrup will
    work as well

½ cup (4 ounces) creamy
    peanut butter

1½ cups full-fat buttermilk, cold

3 tablespoons salted butter,
    melted

The *Soul Food Cookbook* has a bevy of recipes that showcase both Pamela's culinary artistry and her southern roots. My favorite is one for peanut butter biscuits. The very idea of putting peanut butter into the biscuit mix had never crossed my mind. Her recipe uses just 2 tablespoons of peanut butter in a baking soda biscuit. I've built onto that to add more peanut butter flavor. So, when you add a little jelly, the classic PB&J takes on a new form.

1. Adjust the oven rack to the middle position and preheat the oven to 450°F.

2. Place the flour, brown sugar, baking powder, salt, baking soda, and cinnamon in a large bowl and whisk to combine.

3. Place 2 tablespoons of the cane syrup and the peanut butter in a small bowl and whisk to combine. Add the peanut butter mixture to the dry ingredients, using your fingers to distribute it evenly.

4. Add the buttermilk and stir gently with a spatula until the dough forms into a ball and no dry bits of flour are visible. The dough will be shaggy and sticky.

5. Turn the dough out onto a lightly floured surface and lightly dust with flour. With floured hands, pat the dough into a ½-inch-thick 11 × 6-inch rectangle. Fold the ends of the rectangle toward the center, one end on top of the other, to create a trifold. Dust the top lightly with flour, press out to the same size rectangle again, and repeat the folding. Repeat this process a third time. After the third folding, pat the dough to a ½-inch thickness and cut out the biscuits using a floured 2½-inch biscuit cutter. Be careful to press straight down and do not twist the cutter.

6. Place the biscuit rounds 1 inch apart on a parchment-lined baking sheet. Gather the scraps, reshape them, and pat them out to a ½-inch thickness. Cut out as above. Discard any remaining scraps.

7. Bake for 15 to 17 minutes, rotating the pan once halfway through, until the tops are golden brown.

8. Place the remaining 1 tablespoon cane syrup and melted butter in a small bowl and whisk until combined. Brush the tops of the biscuits with the mixture when they come out of the oven and serve warm.

# S'mores Biscuits

**YIELD: 8 TO 10 BISCUITS**

1½ cups / 180 grams
    all-purpose flour, plus extra
    for folding and cutting
1 cup / 143 grams Anson Mills
    graham flour
1 tablespoon baking powder
½ teaspoon baking soda
½ teaspoon kosher salt
½ cup (4 ounces) semisweet
    chocolate chips
1 stick (8 tablespoons) unsalted
    butter, cold
1½ cups full-fat buttermilk, cold
1 cup marshmallow crème

When I decided to write a cookbook, my mother made me promise not to add recipes with ingredients she couldn't buy at Piggly Wiggly. While I think I've done my best, this recipe calls for graham flour, so she'll more than likely roll her eyes when she reads it. Graham flour is a coarse-ground wheat flour that has a nutty, slightly sweet flavor. Known for making graham crackers, it's also used in pie crust, bread, and biscuits to bring a bit of that graham cracker taste.

These graham biscuits have bits of chocolate in each bite. When they are hot out of the oven, slice them and add a dollop of marshmallow fluff in the center. Those Little Debbie snack cakes ain't got nothing on these.

1. Adjust the oven rack to the middle position and preheat the oven to 450°F.

2. Place the all-purpose flour, graham flour, baking powder, baking soda, and salt in a large bowl and whisk to combine. Add the chocolate chips and toss to coat.

3. Using the slicing side of a box grater, slice the butter into the flour mixture. Toss the sheets of butter in the flour.

4. Place the biscuit mixture into the freezer for 15 minutes.

5. Add the buttermilk and stir gently with a spatula until the dough forms into a ball and no dry bits of flour are visible. The dough will be shaggy and sticky.

6. Turn the dough onto a lightly floured surface and lightly dust with flour. With floured hands, pat the dough into a ½-inch-thick 11 × 6-inch rectangle. Fold the ends of the rectangle toward the center, one end on top of the other, to create a trifold. Dust the top lightly with flour, pat out to the same size rectangle again, and repeat the folding. Repeat this process a third time. After the third folding, pat the dough to a ½-inch thickness and cut out the biscuits using a floured 2½-inch biscuit cutter. Be careful to press straight down and do not twist the cutter.

7. Place the biscuit rounds 1 inch apart on a parchment-lined baking sheet. Gather the scraps, reshape them, and pat them out to a ½-inch thickness. Cut out as above. Discard any remaining scraps. Place the baking sheet with the cut biscuits into the freezer for 15 minutes.

8. Remove the pan from the freezer and bake for 15 to 17 minutes, rotating the pan once halfway through, until the tops are golden brown.

9. To serve, slice the biscuits in half and smear the bottom halves with marshmallow crème. Top with the biscuit tops and serve warm.

# Cinnamon Sugar and Pecan Biscuits

YIELD: 12 TO 14 BISCUITS

### CINNAMON SUGAR TOPPING

2 tablespoons sugar
1 teaspoon ground cinnamon

### BISCUITS

2½ cups / 300 grams all-purpose flour, plus extra for rolling and cutting
1 tablespoon baking powder
1¼ teaspoons kosher salt
½ teaspoon baking soda
2 tablespoons vegetable shortening, cold
1 stick (8 tablespoons) unsalted butter, cold
½ cup chopped pecans
1¼ cups full-fat buttermilk, cold
2 tablespoons salted butter, melted

Mr. Zeke and his pecan trees lived across the street from my granny growing up. He kept the entire neighborhood well supplied with pecans. In return, an endless supply of pecan desserts came from my granny's kitchen. These biscuits bake up with a sandy sugar-crunch top that crumbles like my favorite cereal, Cinnamon Toast Crunch. Bits of pecan add a slightly smoky, buttery flavor.

1. Adjust the oven rack to the middle position and preheat the oven to 450°F.

2. For the cinnamon sugar topping: Place the sugar and cinnamon in a small bowl and whisk to combine. Set aside.

3. For the biscuits: Place the flour, baking powder, salt, and baking soda in a large bowl and whisk to combine.

4. Using your fingers, a pastry cutter, or a fork, work the shortening into the flour mixture until only pea-sized pieces of shortening remain. Using the slicing side of a box grater, slice the butter into the flour mixture. Toss the sheets of butter in the flour and then lightly work the butter pieces between your fingers or use a pastry cutter to break them up and coat them with flour. Stop when the dough resembles coarse sand and there are still some small visible pieces of butter.

5. Place the biscuit mix into the freezer for 15 minutes.

6. Gently toss in the chopped pecans. Add the buttermilk and stir gently with a spatula until the dough forms into a ball and no dry bits of flour are visible. The dough will be shaggy and sticky.

7. Turn the dough onto a lightly floured surface and lightly dust with flour. With floured hands, pat the dough into a ½-inch-thick 11 × 6-inch rectangle. Fold the ends of the rectangle toward the center, one end on top of the other, to create a trifold. Dust the top lightly with flour, press out to the same size rectangle again, and repeat the folding. Repeat this process a third time. After the third folding, pat the dough to a ½-inch thickness and cut with a floured 2½-inch biscuit cutter. Be careful to press straight down and do not twist the cutter.

8. Place the biscuit rounds 1 inch apart on a parchment-lined baking sheet. Gather the scraps, reshape them, and pat them out to a ½-inch thickness. Cut out as above. Discard any remaining scraps.

9. Brush the tops of the biscuits with the melted butter and sprinkle with the cinnamon sugar topping.

10. Bake for 12 to 15 minutes, rotating the pan once halfway through, until the tops are golden brown. Serve immediately.

*Still We Rise*

# Whole Wheat Maple Oat Biscuits

**YIELD: 6 TO 8 BISCUITS**

1½ cups / 230 grams whole wheat flour, plus extra for folding and cutting
¼ cup powdered milk
1 tablespoon baking powder
1½ teaspoons kosher salt
½ cup old-fashioned rolled oats
¼ cup plus 2 tablespoons maple syrup
¾ cup full-fat buttermilk, cold

In her cookbook *In the Pursuit of Flavor*, the iconic southern chef Edna Lewis opens the chapter on breads talking about flour and her preference for unbleached over the now standardized, chemical-laden flours that are mostly sold commercially. Lewis details how her family threshed their own wheat, took it to the mill, and had it ground, and she encourages the reader to try out different types of flour. This inspired my own journey of experimentation with different flours to make biscuits. For this recipe, you'll need whole wheat flour rather than the all-purpose that we've been using, creating a coarser biscuit with a nutty flavor. We also add hearty oats and hints of maple. Valerie's Apple Butter (page 152) will add both sweetness and a taste of fall. My husband will tell you that this biscuit topped with an over easy egg and a generous smear of Hominy Honey Butter (page 150) makes for a wholesome breakfast on a cold morning.

1. Adjust the oven rack to the middle position and preheat the oven to 450°F.

2. Place the flour, powdered milk, baking powder, and salt in a large bowl and whisk to combine.

3. Add the oats and ¼ cup of the maple syrup to a small bowl and toss until well combined. Add the oat mixture to the flour mixture and stir to combine.

4. Add the buttermilk and stir gently with a spatula until the dough forms into a ball and no dry bits of flour are visible. The dough will be shaggy and sticky.

5. Turn the dough onto a lightly floured surface and lightly dust with flour. With floured hands, pat the dough into a ½-inch-thick 11 × 6-inch rectangle. Fold the ends of the rectangle toward the center, one end on top of the other, to create a trifold. Dust the top lightly with flour, press out to the same size rectangle again, and repeat the folding. Repeat this process a third time. After the third folding, pat the dough to a ½-inch thickness and cut out the biscuits using a floured 2½-inch biscuit cutter. Be careful to press straight down and do not twist the cutter.

6. Place the biscuit rounds 1 inch apart on a parchment-lined baking sheet. Gather the scraps, reshape them, and pat them out to a ½-inch thickness. Cut out as above. Discard any remaining scraps. Brush the tops of the biscuits with the remaining 2 tablespoons maple syrup.

7. Bake for 12 to 15 minutes, rotating the pan once halfway through, until the tops are light golden brown. Serve immediately.

# 7.

# SPREAD LOVE LIKE BUTTER

*Jams, Spreads, and Butters to Jazz Up Your Biscuits*

# Blackberry Jam

YIELD: ABOUT 1 QUART

2 pounds blackberries
2 cups sugar
Zest and juice of 1 lemon
1 teaspoon ground cinnamon
1 teaspoon ground nutmeg
½ teaspoon kosher salt

*We didn't have very big breakfasts on school days when I was growing up. It was usually just a biscuit and strawberry or blackberry jam.*
   —Leah Chase, *The Dooky Chase Cookbook*

Several times a week, my breakfast of choice consists of biscuits and whatever jam I have on hand at the time. One of summer's simple pleasures is blackberries, which make one of my favorite jams. Fresh lemon juice and zest bring out the flavor in the berries, making this spread truly magnificent. Blackberries and corn are one of summer's tastiest flavor combinations, so I recommend using this jam on a Cornmeal Cream Biscuit (page 114) or Corn Milk Biscuit (page 111).

1. In a large, heavy-bottomed pot over medium heat, combine the blackberries, sugar, lemon zest and juice, cinnamon, nutmeg, and salt and bring the mixture to a boil. Decrease the heat to medium-low and cook, stirring frequently, until the jam thickens and coats the back of a spoon. Set aside to cool completely, about 1½ hours.

2. Transfer to an airtight container and store in the refrigerator for up to 2 weeks or the freezer for up to 2 months.

# Georgia Peach Mango Jam

YIELD: ABOUT 2 CUPS

2 pounds (about 4 large) peaches, peeled and chopped

2 large mangoes, peeled and chopped (about 3 cups)

1½ cups sugar

¼ cup freshly squeezed lemon juice

I never knew much about peaches other than that I could eat a whole basketful if left to my own devices. When I moved to Atlanta, it was the middle of summer and our next-door neighbor had a peach tree in the backyard. Upon our first meeting, he decided he was going to teach me all about peaches. He taught me about every variety of peach, when to grow them, which kind worked best for jams versus eating—to the point that I would go to the farmers' market feeling like a peach expert.

This jam is simple, with peaches taking center stage. The bright and acidic taste of a juicy peach married with the slightly floral, almost evergreen taste of mangoes makes this one of my favorite jams. Enjoy these with the milky soft Fellowship Hall Biscuits (page 51). Praise the Lord and pass the biscuits.

1. In a large, heavy-bottomed saucepan over medium-high heat, combine the peaches, mangoes, sugar, and lemon juice and bring the mixture to a boil. Decrease the heat to medium and cook, stirring frequently, until the fruit is softened and reduced by almost half, about 20 minutes.

2. Remove from the heat and blend with an immersion blender for a smooth consistency or mash with a potato masher for a chunkier consistency.

3. Return the jam to medium heat and continue to cook, stirring continuously, until the mixture has thickened enough to coat the back of a spoon, another 6 to 8 minutes.

4. Set aside to cool completely. Transfer to an airtight container and store in the refrigerator for up to 2 weeks or the freezer for up to 2 months.

# Blueberry Lemon Jam

YIELD: ABOUT 1 QUART

8 cups (38 ounces) fresh or
   frozen blueberries
2 cups sugar
Zest and juice of 1 lemon

A close friend and I once took a road trip to Washington, D.C., for the Howard University homecoming, which was not to be missed. On the way, we stopped at her aunt's house in Virginia. It was late when we arrived, but she had hot plates waiting for us on the dining room table. Aunt Mel, as she was called, had a painting on her wall that showed three Black women dressed in white. Bluish-purple stains streaked their skirts. Brimmed straw hats adorned their heads, and large buckets laid at their feet. They were surrounded by fields of berry-studded bushes that appeared to be blowing in the wind. It was mesmerizing. All Black aunties and grandmas have some form of Black art on the walls of their house, but I'd yet to see anything like this. Aunt Mel didn't remember where the painting came from, but it reminded her of the women who long ago used to work the blueberry fields in North Carolina. She told us about the buses coming and picking up people as early as 4:00 a.m. back in the 1930s. They would be paid at the end of the day after working from sunup to sundown. In some cases, housing was located right on the farm where they worked, "housing" meaning shacks of several people. Sheets with hues of blues and reds were hung out to dry, showing the stains of their labor.

Blueberries are juicy and sweet with a slightly acidic flavor. Some of the smaller varieties have an almost floral taste. The lemon added to the blueberries while cooking adds a slight tartness to the jam and helps intensify the blueberry flavor. Slather this jam across the Peanut Butter and Cane Syrup Biscuits (page 137) for a next-level PB&J.

1. In a heavy-bottomed 4-quart saucepan over medium heat, combine the blueberries, sugar, and lemon zest and juice. Stir and bring to a boil. Cook, stirring constantly, until the jam thickens and coats the back of a spoon, 30 to 35 minutes. Set aside to cool completely, about 1 hour.

2. Transfer to an airtight container and store in the refrigerator for up to 2 weeks or the freezer for up to 2 months.

# Tomato Jam

**YIELD: ABOUT 1½ CUPS**

1½ pounds Roma tomatoes,
    finely chopped
½ cup granulated sugar
½ cup packed dark brown sugar
2 tablespoons freshly squeezed
    lemon juice
1 teaspoon kosher salt
½ teaspoon ground cumin
¼ teaspoon ground cinnamon

A little slather of tomato jam jazzes up any biscuit. My great-aunt Mabel would stew tomatoes she grew in her backyard, adding them to soups and freezing some for later. She seemed to always have tomatoes, so I assumed they grew year-round until I was old enough to know better. I don't stew tomatoes quite like she did, but I can make one hell of a batch of jam out of them.

Tomato jam is an enchanting spread to me. The process starts out like you're making a glorious tomato sauce but results in a sweet and slightly sour jammy spread that is outstanding on everything from buttermilk biscuits to a BLT.

1. In a heavy-bottomed 4-quart saucepan over medium-high heat, combine the tomatoes, granulated and brown sugars, lemon juice, salt, cumin, and cinnamon and bring the mixture to a boil, stirring occasionally. Decrease the heat to low and cook, uncovered, stirring continually to prevent scorching, until the mixture has reduced by half, 40 to 45 minutes.

2. Remove from the heat and let cool completely before using, Transfer to an airtight container and store in the refrigerator for up to 2 weeks or the freezer for up to 2 months.

*Still We Rise*

# Hominy Honey Butter

**YIELD: ABOUT 2 CUPS**

1 cup canned cooked hominy, drained
2 sticks (1 cup) salted butter, room temperature
½ teaspoon kosher salt
6 tablespoons honey
Zest and juice of 1 lemon

This hominy butter is one of the many creations that Mike Sheats, longtime pop-up collaborator, has whipped up for events. The first time was to go along with some roasted pork loin biscuit sandwiches. One spoonful smeared over a hot biscuit, and I was a believer.

Hominy comes from field corn, which is also used to make tortillas. It has a nutty corn flavor. When cooked, it's earthy with a soft, creamy texture that is similar to grits or polenta. This recipe mixes hominy and salted butter with honey for a hint of sweetness, making it taste like spreadable popcorn. Make a batch of Butter Swim Biscuits (page 73) to spread this butter on, and you won't be disappointed.

1. In the bowl of a food processor, place the hominy, butter, salt, honey, and lemon zest and juice and process until smooth, stopping to scrape down the sides of the bowl once or twice, 1 to 2 minutes.

2. Transfer the mixture to an airtight container and refrigerate overnight before using. Store refrigerated for up to 2 weeks.

# Cantaloupe Butter

YIELD: ABOUT 2½ CUPS

3½ to 4 pounds cantaloupe
2 cups sugar
½ cup freshly squeezed lemon
  juice (about 3 lemons)
1 teaspoon ground cinnamon
1 teaspoon ground ginger
1 teaspoon ground allspice
1 teaspoon ground berbere
1 teaspoon vanilla extract

In Patty Pinner's 2004 cookbook, *Sweets: A Collection of Soul Food Desserts and Memories*, she shares stories of growing up in a large family in Michigan where she helped the women of the house make fabulous sweets that they would show off at church and neighborhood gatherings. You can't help but feel connected to her relatives as you cook your way through the book. One recipe is for Aunt Pinky's cantaloupe pie, which calls for boiling cantaloupe with sugar until the melon is soft and tender, then mashing it with a fork to make the filling for the pie. It was the first recipe I baked from her book because I'd grown up eating boiled cantaloupe, which is delicious. If you've never tried it, it is mild and sweet, with a honey-like flavor.

Cantaloupe butter is the even more intense version, concentrating the flavor of melon with cinnamon and lots of sugar. I also add berbere, a traditional Ethiopian blend of chili peppers, ginger, allspice, and other warm spices. The results hardly resemble cantaloupe. This fruit butter has a rich brown color and at first glance looks like apple butter.

1. Clean, seed, and cut the cantaloupe flesh into chunks. Place the chunks into a blender and puree until smooth.

2. In a heavy-bottomed 4-quart saucepan over medium-high heat, combine the pureed cantaloupe, sugar, lemon juice, cinnamon, ginger, allspice, and berbere and bring the mixture to a boil, stirring occasionally. Decrease the heat to medium-low and cook, uncovered, stirring frequently to prevent scorching, until the mixture has reduced by half and reaches 217°F on an instant-read thermometer, 25 to 30 minutes.

3. Remove from the heat, stir in the vanilla, and let cool completely before using. Transfer to an airtight container and store in the refrigerator for up to 2 weeks or the freezer for up to 2 months.

# Valerie's Apple Butter

YIELD: ABOUT 3 CUPS

3 pounds apples, peeled, cored, and cut into ½-inch-cubes
1 cup sugar
1½ teaspoons ground cinnamon
1 teaspoon kosher salt
¼ teaspoon freshly grated nutmeg
¼ teaspoon ground cloves
¼ teaspoon ground ginger
1 teaspoon vanilla extract

Red Delicious, Gala, Fuji, and McIntosh apples all work well in this recipe. I've tossed one or two Granny Smiths in the bunch a few times as well. The sugar and spice balance out the tartness. For me, apple butter can be eaten straight out of the jar with a spoon, but spreading some across a warm buttermilk biscuit is my preferred method to enjoy this sweet, spiced spread. You can also add a dollop or two over pancakes and waffles, stir it into a bowl of oatmeal, or even brush some on roasting chicken during the last few minutes of cooking. Apple butter can enhance the flavor profile of almost any dish.

1. Place the apples, sugar, cinnamon, salt, nutmeg, cloves, and ginger into a heavy-bottomed 6-quart pot and stir to combine. Set over medium heat and stir frequently until the sugar dissolves and the apples begin to give up some of their juices, about 10 minutes. Decrease the heat to medium-low, cover, and cook, removing the lid and stirring every 15 to 20 minutes, until the apples break down and the mixture thickens slightly, about 1 hour.

2. Uncover, add the vanilla, and stir to combine. Cook, stirring frequently, until the mixture is thick and darkens in color, another 20 minutes.

3. Remove from the heat and use an immersion blender to puree until smooth.

4. Transfer the mixture to an airtight container and store in the refrigerator for up to 2 weeks or the freezer for up to 2 months.

## Apple Butter Love

Valerie Boyd had a regal, quiet presence. A longtime journalist and author, she ran the MFA program in journalism at the University of Georgia. She was also a dear friend and mentor. To spend the day sitting on the screened-in porch at her house by the lake in Georgia was the most tranquil experience, one that made you feel like you were miles away from anything that didn't bring you peace. We met at a conference by Southern Foodways Alliance, an organization that celebrates the food culture of the South. It was an honor to spend an evening laughing like old friends over pizza. We promised to keep in contact, and that we did.

Valerie would patronize a lot of my pop-ups going forward. When I decided to write a cookbook, I was told that books on biscuits already existed (and all were written by white women). When I told Valerie this, her response was "What's that got to do with the book you're going to write?" Valerie guided me through the journey of writing, helping me find the way to put my voice on paper. *Still We Rise* bears her mark because those were her words to me.

In the summer of 2019, Valerie invited me to Eatonton, Georgia, to discuss taking part in birthday celebrations for Alice Walker. When the details were finalized, I was to make breakfast for Walker at an event she was hosting for a few select local college students. When I met her a few months later, I felt like I was floating. Over the years, Valerie would introduce me to a wonderful group of people who would go on to support me in this biscuit business—kind people who exuded the same warmth that she did. Valerie's recommendation was always "You must try Erika's apple butter," so I'd make sure I had it when she was coming by or when I visited. Once I told her how my granny made it. It's a simple recipe that just requires the apples to cook down slowly. Val told me that all things that take time are more precious and that the love I felt for my granny fills my spirit when I make it.

I'll always be grateful for Valerie's presence in my life, and I still have a tough time accepting she is no longer here to sit on the porch to eat biscuits and apple butter with. Those memories will live with me always. Each batch of apple butter I make now carries the spirit of both Granny Geraldine and Valerie, making it all the sweeter.

# Strawberry Butter

YIELD: ABOUT 2 CUPS

2 sticks (1 cup) salted butter,
   room temperature
½ cup powdered sugar
½ cup (2 ounces) fresh
   strawberries, tops removed
¼ teaspoon ground ginger
Zest of 1 lemon

Listen, this butter should come with a warning because it's addictive—sweet, creamy, and pink with fresh strawberry puree. I've got a customer who comes into the restaurant and asks for it every week in the hope I'll say, "Yep, we've got some today." Sometimes I'll feel bad about not making it because I know he'll be there, so I will make just a small batch, hide it in the fridge, and pass it to him when no one is looking. Like a strawberry butter dealer. Now you can make this at home and enjoy the fruit butters of your labor smeared over biscuits, pancakes, and even cinnamon rolls. We really put this spread on everything.

1. In the bowl of a food processor, place the butter, powdered sugar, strawberries, ginger, and lemon zest and process until smooth, stopping to scrape down the sides of the bowl once or twice, 1 to 2 minutes.

2. Transfer the mixture to an airtight container and refrigerate overnight before using. Store refrigerated for up to 2 weeks.

# Cheerwine Mustard

YIELD: ½ CUP

¼ cup ground mustard powder
2 tablespoons whole brown
  mustard seeds
1 teaspoon salt
¼ cup Cheerwine
1 tablespoon apple cider
  vinegar

Cheerwine is a North Carolina staple, and while I now reside in Atlanta, some habits are just hard to break. Cheerwine has nothing to do with wine, and although it is the color of merlot, it's a sweet, dark cherry–flavored cola that, in North Carolina, we think pairs well with everything. It's often the secret ingredient in some folks' baked beans and even BBQ. I've added some Cheerwine to mustard for a sweet-hot spread, perfect on a Pretzel Biscuit (page 69) with a smoked sausage link.

If you have no luck finding Cheerwine in your area, try Cherry Coke or Dr Pepper.

1. Place the mustard powder, mustard seeds, and salt in a small bowl and whisk to combine.

2. Add the Cheerwine and vinegar and whisk to combine. The mixture will be very thin. Cover the bowl with plastic wrap or a lid and refrigerate for 24 hours.

3. Remove the plastic and stir to combine. The mixture will have thickened. Transfer to an airtight container and refrigerate until ready to use. It will keep in the refrigerator for up to 1 month.

# Dynamite Sauce

YIELD: ABOUT 1 CUP

½ cup Duke's mayonnaise
3 tablespoons ketchup
2 tablespoons hot sauce
2 tablespoons pickle juice
1 teaspoon Worcestershire
  sauce
½ teaspoon garlic powder
¼ teaspoon cayenne pepper
¼ teaspoon freshly ground
  black pepper

Dynamite Sauce is very similar to the traditional southern comeback sauce. Comeback sauce originated in Mississippi. A mixture of mayo, ketchup, and spices, it has a flavor close to Louisiana remoulade or Thousand Island dressing without the sweetness. At Bomb Biscuit Co., we decided to blend up our own spin. Dynamite Sauce has the same base of mayo and ketchup, but I added the magical power of pickle juice and hot sauce for more POW and depth of flavor. We use Dynamite Sauce on everything from crispy hash browns to fried catfish or oyster biscuit sandwiches. Up the cayenne pepper and add in a teaspoon or two of red pepper flakes if you want some extra heat.

1. Place the mayonnaise, ketchup, hot sauce, pickle juice, Worcestershire sauce, garlic powder, cayenne pepper, and black pepper in a medium bowl and whisk to combine.

2. Store in an airtight container in the refrigerator for up to 2 weeks.

# Deviled Ham

**YIELD: ABOUT 2 CUPS**

8 ounces (about 2 cups) cooked ham, diced

¼ cup Duke's mayonnaise

2 teaspoons yellow mustard

2 teaspoons Texas Pete hot sauce

1 teaspoon garlic powder

1 teaspoon freshly ground black pepper

½ teaspoon paprika

½ teaspoon cayenne pepper

¼ cup finely chopped yellow onion

¼ cup finely chopped celery

This is a little throwback spread to add to your hot biscuit. As a kid, I used to ask why things were called "deviled" anything, mainly because of the deviled eggs we ate every Easter. Granny would laugh and say you scoop the cooked egg yolks into a bowl and beat the devil out of them. That doesn't really apply here, as it calls for the use of a food processor, and telling one to pulse the devil out of the ingredients doesn't sound as catchy. This spread may be a tough sell for those who remember the odd-colored deviled ham in a can of yesteryear (even though I LOVE that stuff). This recipe has a bit more of a chunky texture, and the cayenne and hot sauce add a little heat. Depending on the ham used, there may be a hint of sweetness. Country ham, which is cured in salt, will make this spread a little too salty, so let's save that for another recipe. Deviled ham tastes great sandwiched, especially on a Sour Cream and Onion Biscuit (page 99). I highly recommend you try it.

1. In the bowl of a food processor, place the ham, mayonnaise, mustard, hot sauce, garlic powder, black pepper, paprika, and cayenne and pulse until the mixture is slightly chunky and spreadable, 15 to 20 pulses.

2. Transfer to a bowl, add the onion and celery, and stir to combine. Serve immediately or store in an airtight container in the refrigerator for up to 1 week.

# Pimento Cheese

YIELD: ABOUT 2¼ CUPS

8 ounces (about 2 cups)
shredded extra-sharp
cheddar cheese

8 ounces cream cheese, room
temperature

4-ounce jar pimentos, drained

½ cup Duke's mayonnaise

1 tablespoon dried parsley

1 teaspoon kosher salt, plus
extra as needed

½ teaspoon freshly ground
black pepper, plus extra as
needed

¼ teaspoon garlic powder

¼ teaspoon cayenne pepper
(optional)

Pimento cheese is a classic southern spread that combines cream cheese, cheddar cheese, and pimento peppers. It is sometimes referred to as "the southern pâté." Depending on who makes it, it can come with a kick of heat. William Thomas Council, a.k.a. my dad, will tell you that he makes the best pimento cheese in the world. Yes, the world. He's truly humble like that. He's had my pimento cheese, which, of course, *I* think is the best and which he'll say is "really good and close, but not quite like mine."

We have this sort of back-and-forth banter on pimento cheese and bourbon. One thing he will concede is that my griddled pimento cheese on a biscuit is truly something special. In this recipe, the sharp cheddar cheese peppers up the cream cheese base with its nuttiness, and the mayo adds a taste of butter.

We griddle the cheese spread just enough to get it melting and then scoop it on top of sausage or fried chicken. It makes for a heavenly experience and will require a nap after consuming. I'll show you how to do this at home, but first you need to make the pimento cheese. It's really good and close, but not quite like William Council's.

1. In the bowl of a stand mixer, place the cheddar, cream cheese, pimentos, mayonnaise, parsley, salt, black pepper, garlic powder, and cayenne pepper (if using). Using the paddle attachment, beat on medium speed until thoroughly combined, 1 to 2 minutes, stopping to scrape down the sides of the bowl as needed. Taste and adjust the seasoning as desired with salt and pepper.

2. Refrigerate in an airtight container until ready to serve. Store refrigerated for up to 1 week.

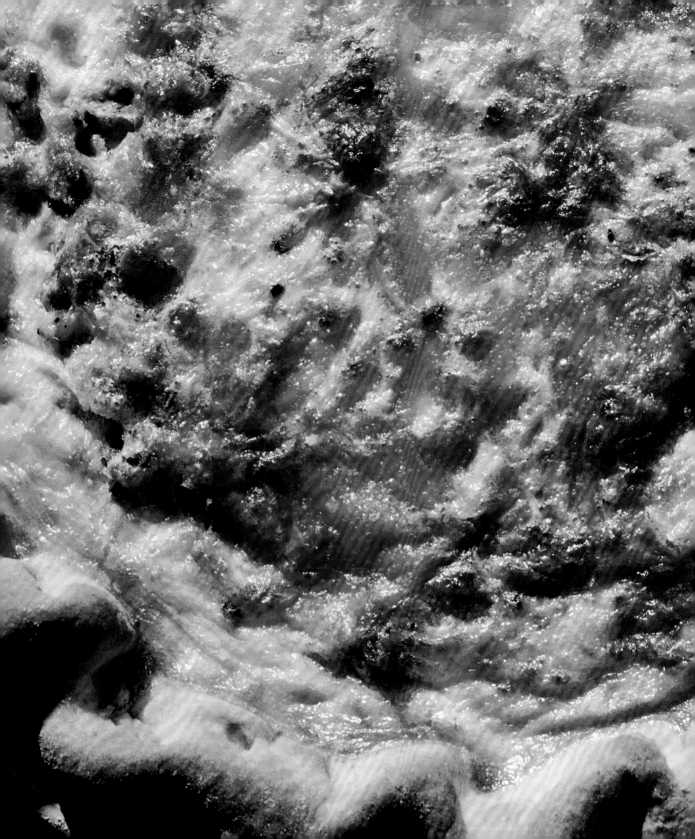

# 8.

# BISCUIT BREAKFAST AND BRUNCH

# Southern Aloha Biscuit Sandwich

YIELD: 4 SANDWICHES

8 ounces sliced country ham

4 large eggs, beaten

Salt and freshly ground black pepper, to taste

4 slices muenster or Gouda cheese

3 tablespoons honey

2 tablespoons salted butter, melted

4 Hawaiian Sweet Biscuits (page 129)

In the fall of 2021, after years of pop-ups, farmers' market tents, and running deliveries around the city of Atlanta, we finally moved Bomb Biscuit Co. into a permanent brick-and-mortar location in the Old Fourth Ward district of Atlanta. At first, I wasn't sure what to expect because, while I'd found unexpected success in all the prior iterations of my biscuit-baking vocation, having an actual restaurant was never in the plan. So, with a roll of the proverbial dice and a quick prayer, I turned the "We're Open" sign on at our little 450-square-foot space with just me and two other employees. We somehow churned out thousands of biscuits in that little closet-sized bakery in the span of just six months, to the point that we had to expand into the other area of the market space we occupied. With that came the expansion of our menu. In this chapter, we'll be making some of Bomb Biscuit Co.'s customer-favorite biscuit sandwiches.

Each week we run a sandwich special at the restaurant. Often, I'll look at the biscuits that sell the best and build a sandwich based on them, like the Hawaiian Sweet Biscuits. We kept getting requests to add bacon or even fried chicken to these bite-sized biscuits. The sweetness of the honey-topped biscuits had me thinking of my favorite sandwich, the Monte Cristo, which is made with butter-crisped bread, ham, and melted cheese and dusted with powdered sugar (a "ham and cheese doughnut," as my son calls it). So, we decided to try out our own version. The salty smokiness of country ham draped with melting muenster cheese, sandwiched on a honey-glazed biscuit, is a euphoric delight and one of our most popular specials.

1. In a medium skillet over medium heat, add the country ham slices and cook until heated through, 1 to 2 minutes on each side. Remove the ham and set aside in a warm oven until ready to build the sandwich.

2. Spray the skillet with nonstick cooking spray. Add the eggs and cook until almost set, seasoning with salt and pepper as desired. Divide the eggs into 4 equal parts in the pan and top each portion with a slice of cheese and continue to cook until the eggs are set and the cheese has melted slightly.

3. Place the honey and melted butter in a small bowl and whisk to combine.

4. Cut the biscuits in half and reheat if necessary (see Cook's Note). Divide the country ham among the biscuit bottoms and top with the cheese, eggs, and biscuit top. Brush the tops with the honey mixture and serve immediately.

*Cook's Note: If you are not making the sandwiches the same day, brush the cut biscuits with melted butter and reheat, cut side down, in a skillet or sauté pan over medium heat for 1 to 2 minutes.*

# Country Ham and Pimento Cheese on a Cornmeal Biscuit, a.k.a. Big Country Biscuit

**YIELD: 4 SANDWICHES**

8 ounces sliced country ham
1 cup Pimento Cheese
   (page 161)
4 Chive and Red Pepper
   Cornmeal Biscuits
   (page 113)

As a teenager, I worked at a popular biscuit place where club soda was added to the biscuit mix, which was then kneaded in a Hobart commercial mixer. It took two of us to get the bowl off the mixer and pour what felt like five hundred pounds of dough onto a counter. One of the most popular sandwiches on the menu was country ham. This isn't surprising since one of the key industries of North Carolina is hog farming, so pork is a big part of the state's foodways.

Country ham is a heavily salted ham that's preserved by curing and smoking. The pimento cheese for this sandwich is warmed up a bit to get it slightly melty, but you can also just scoop the cold pimento cheese right onto the sandwich if you prefer.

1. In a medium skillet over medium-high heat, add the country ham slices and cook until heated through, 1 to 2 minutes on each side. Remove the ham and set aside in a warm oven until ready to build the sandwich.

2. Spray the skillet with nonstick cooking spray. Divide the pimento cheese into four 2-ounce scoops and sauté over medium heat until golden and crispy, 1 to 2 minutes. Flip and cook until crispy, 1 to 2 more minutes.

3. Cut the biscuits in half and reheat if necessary (see Cook's Note). To build the sandwich, divide the country ham among the biscuit bottoms and top with the pimento cheese and biscuit top. Serve immediately.

*Cook's Note: If you are not making the sandwiches the same day, brush the cut biscuits with melted butter and reheat, cut side down, in a skillet or sauté pan over medium heat for 1 to 2 minutes.*

*Still We Rise*

# The Glori-Fried Chicken Biscuit Sandwich

**YIELD: 4 SANDWICHES**

1 cup full-fat buttermilk, cold

4 tablespoons Texas Pete hot sauce

1 tablespoon bread-and-butter pickle juice

Four 5- to 7-ounce boneless skinless chicken thighs

¾ cup / 96 grams self-rising flour

2 teaspoons cornstarch

1½ teaspoons kosher salt

1½ teaspoons Tony Chachere's seasoning blend (or any Cajun seasoning)

½ teaspoon paprika

½ teaspoon onion powder

½ teaspoon garlic powder

½ teaspoon freshly ground black pepper

Peanut oil, for frying

3 tablespoons unsalted butter, melted

1 tablespoon honey

4 Bomb Buttermilk Biscuits (page 33)

8 bread-and-butter pickle slices

Saying I make a lot of these biscuits is an understatement. Atlanta loves fried chicken, and I love all y'all that keep coming back for more.

Using chicken thighs (dark meat) helps to make sure you don't serve up dry fried chicken. Nobody likes that. If dark meat is not your thing, I get it and you can switch it out for chicken breast. However, keep in mind that white meat does not take as long to cook as dark, so you will want to check the internal temperature on the chicken a little sooner than the instructions below dictate.

A drizzle of honey butter is a heavenly addition to top off the fried chicken; add a little or a lot to suit your preference.

1. Place the buttermilk, hot sauce, and pickle juice in a medium bowl and whisk to combine. Add the chicken thighs and coat thoroughly with the mixture. Cover and refrigerate for 24 hours, tossing occasionally.

2. Using a slotted spoon, remove the chicken from the marinade and set aside to drain slightly.

3. Place the flour, cornstarch, salt, seasoning blend, paprika, onion powder, garlic powder, and pepper in a small bowl and whisk to combine. Dredge the chicken thighs in the mixture, coating them evenly, and set aside. Place a cooling rack over a paper towel–lined baking sheet.

4. In a 6-quart Dutch oven or heavy-bottomed pot over medium high heat, heat 1½ inches of oil to 325°F. Gently add 2 of the chicken thighs and cook until golden brown and the internal temperature is 165°F, 6 to 7 minutes, turning over halfway through. Transfer the cooked chicken to the cooling rack and repeat with the remaining 2 chicken thighs.

5. Place the melted butter and honey in a small bowl and whisk to combine.

6. Cut the biscuits in half and reheat if necessary (see Cook's Note). To build the sandwich, place 2 pickles on each biscuit bottom, top with the chicken thighs, and drizzle each sandwich evenly with the honey butter mixture. Cover with the biscuit tops and serve immediately.

*Cook's Note: If you are not making the sandwiches the same day, brush the cut biscuits with melted butter and reheat, cut side down, in a skillet or sauté pan over medium heat for 1 to 2 minutes.*

# Glori-Fried

*My mother paid for this place with chicken legs.*

—Belle Winston

Psyche Williams-Forson's book *Building Houses out of Chicken Legs* examines the extraordinary role chicken has played in the lives of Black women, past and present. In it, Belle Winston recounts being a waiter carrier, one of the women who sold fried chicken, biscuits, and breads to travelers arriving via train in Gordonsville, Virginia, beginning in the 1800s. African Americans being able to sell their food to white travelers was unheard of at the time, and these enterprising women provided Black men and women economic opportunities by drawing upon their cooking skills. My grandmother, Mildred Council, built not only houses out of chicken legs but a foundation for generations of her family to stand on when she opened Mama Dip's Kitchen back in 1976. Elsewhere, food sales held at churches, where ladies brought their best dishes and platters of fried chicken, raised money that funded communities.

Outside of financial gain and community building, there is also comfort in fried chicken. There are many stories of pieces of chicken packed in shoeboxes to feed Black travelers as they made their way to destinations around the country under the cloud of racism and segregation. My great-uncle Charles would tell me about how Big Mama would pack him fried chicken, greens, and biscuits to take with him when he traveled. On one of my last visits with him, he gave me a stack of old photographs, and I found a small black-and-white picture of him in his midtwenties holding his shoebox open, the contents covered in aluminum foil. His face radiates such joy and elation.

My father-in-law, Charles, shared his own memories of the fried chicken his mother would ship to him while he was in the service at Fort Knox in Kentucky. My father-in-law and mother-in-law would pack the same for themselves when they traveled to visit relatives in Sparta, Georgia, from their home in Chester, Pennsylvania, under the glare of Jim Crow. My mother-in-law, Marian, shared similar stories about the shoebox and its contents. "It was not a shoebox size, it would need to be more of a boot size box, so it could hold more. We had chicken that was always wrapped in foil, and slices of cake and things that would keep for a long time," she said.

In my experience, fried chicken has always been presented with the greatest of pride. It takes pride of place at our restaurant, as our bestselling biscuit sandwiches are all filled with fried chicken. Whether it's brined in buttermilk and hot sauce, dipped in hot honey or peach habanero sauce, we keep the flavors—and the glory that is hot fried chicken—popping.

My great Uncle Charles Gavin with his shoebox of food.

Fried chicken has played a role at every dinner table in my life. When the weather was cold, there was always candied yams and greens with fried chicken. When it was hot, there was potato salad and sometimes cold fried chicken at the park. I've seen fried chicken prepared a multitude of ways, even though most of them would never pass the ServSafe course and have me wondering how I'm still here.

Here are a few tips for frying up crispy, juicy, golden fried chicken:

**Buttermilk brine:** Buttermilk is one of the best ways to brine chicken. Growing up, chicken pieces were covered with buttermilk, hot sauce, and other seasonings in a large bowl that sat in the sink while we went to church. Back then, the chicken didn't need twenty-four hours to marinate (or refrigeration, apparently). Just long enough to hear God's word, and upon returning, we tossed it in hot grease. Unlike a salt and water brine, the buttermilk adheres to the chicken, making it easier to dredge in seasoned flour. The acid in the buttermilk also tenderizes the chicken. Hot sauce is added for seasoning and flavor.

**Self-rising flour:** This flour has salt and baking powder added in. It helps with both the flavor and texture of the crust on chicken. I tend to not double dredge or use an egg. Using both the buttermilk brine and the self-rising flour gives me a crisp crust with one coat.

**Oil:** Peanut oil is used for both fried chicken recipes in this book, but you can absolutely use vegetable or canola oil if that's your jam. Peanut oil has a high smoke point (410°F), making it ideal for frying. Make sure your oil is at 325°F and maintain that temp throughout frying.

**Temp that bird:** Unlike a good steak, chicken should never be pink in the center. Always check for doneness by sticking a meat thermometer in the thickest part of each piece. The recipes in this book use chicken thighs, which is dark meat, and it should be cooked to 165°F. Dark meat chicken comes from the thigh and drumstick and is more flavorful and juicy.

**Excess oil:** Place the chicken onto a cooling rack just after removing it from the grease. I see a lot about how draining chicken on a paper towel goes against the cardinal rules of frying. Yes, the paper can cause your chicken to go soggy, as will newspaper and stale bread. However, people have used these items plenty of times and all was well. If you have a cooling rack, I'd suggest using that so the chicken can drain and air can still circulate around it, keeping it dry and crisp. If not, just don't let the chicken linger too long on that paper towel or folks will likely talk about your mushy chicken, and no one wants that.

# Fried Green Tomato Biscuit Sandwich

YIELD: 4 SANDWICHES

½ cup full-fat buttermilk, cold

1 cup / 120 grams all-purpose flour

½ cup / 75 grams stone-ground yellow cornmeal

½ cup / 30 grams panko bread crumbs

2 teaspoons kosher salt

¼ teaspoon freshly ground black pepper

4 green tomatoes, sliced ½ inch thick

Peanut oil or vegetable oil, for frying

1 cup Pimento Cheese (page 161)

4 Bomb Buttermilk Biscuits (page 33)

The glorious golden beauty of fried green tomatoes is one of the best things about southern summers. Unripened tomatoes are soaked in buttermilk and then coated in a seasoned mixture of cornmeal, bread crumbs, and flour, then fried until crisp on each side and still firm but juicy in the middle. They can be enjoyed just as they are, but my preferred way of eating them is sandwiched on a biscuit topped with griddled pimento cheese. These sandwiches can also be served with just a scoop of chilled pimento cheese.

1. Place the buttermilk in a medium bowl. Place the flour, cornmeal, bread crumbs, salt, and pepper in a separate medium bowl.

2. Place each tomato slice into the buttermilk, then dredge it in the flour mixture to completely coat.

3. Add about 1 inch of peanut oil to a large skillet. The amount will vary depending on the size of the skillet you are using. Heat the oil over medium-high heat. Working in batches, place 3 or 4 tomato slices at a time in the skillet, making sure they are not touching. Cook until the tomatoes are golden brown, about 2 to 3 minutes, then flip and fry on the other side, about another 2 to 3 more minutes.

4. Remove from the skillet and transfer to a paper towel–lined plate to drain. Repeat with the remaining tomato slices.

5. Coat a separate skillet with nonstick cooking spray. Divide the pimento cheese into four 2-ounce scoops and sauté until golden and crispy, 1 to 2 minutes. Flip and cook until crispy on the other side, 1 to 2 more minutes.

6. Cut the biscuits in half and reheat if necessary (see Cook's Note). To build the sandwich, place a fried green tomato on the biscuit bottom and top with the pimento cheese and biscuit top. Serve immediately.

*Cook's Note: If you are not making the sandwiches the same day, brush the cut biscuits with melted butter and reheat, cut side down, in a skillet or sauté pan over medium heat for 1 to 2 minutes.*

# Lemon Pepper Chicken Biscuit Sandwich

**YIELD: 4 SANDWICHES**

### FRIED CHICKEN

1 cup full-fat buttermilk, cold

4 tablespoons Texas Pete hot sauce

1 tablespoon bread-and-butter pickle juice

Four 5- to 7-ounce boneless skinless chicken thighs

¾ cup / 90 grams self-rising flour

2 teaspoons cornstarch

1½ teaspoons kosher salt

1½ teaspoons Tony Chachere's seasoning blend (or any Cajun seasoning)

½ teaspoon paprika

½ teaspoon onion powder

½ teaspoon garlic powder

½ teaspoon freshly ground black pepper

Peanut oil, for frying

### LEMON PEPPER BUTTER SAUCE

Zest and juice from 2 lemons

1 teaspoon fresh coarsely ground black pepper

½ teaspoon kosher salt

2 tablespoons unsalted butter, melted

4 Bomb Buttermilk Biscuits (page 33)

8 bread-and-butter pickle slices

"Lemon pepper wet" is my favorite style of wings. Where I grew up, there was a little spot that would toss the wings in the sauce and then dump more on top. The "spot" was actually a shack run by a lady and her son. The menu was taped to the window, and the food was passed to you from the back porch. If you weren't careful, that sauce would drip right onto your lap.

We serve a lemon pepper chicken biscuit with thighs that are tossed in a fresh lemon pepper butter sauce sandwiched on a buttermilk biscuit with bread-and-butter pickles. People were hesitant to try it when we first added it to the menu, unsure of how the lemon pepper seasoning would mix with a biscuit, but once they tried it, they were forever converted. We often find ourselves running out of lemon pepper seasoning because people even ask for it on the side.

1. For the chicken: Place the buttermilk, hot sauce, and pickle juice in a medium bowl and whisk to combine. Add the chicken thighs and coat thoroughly with the mixture. Cover and refrigerate for 24 hours, tossing occasionally.

2. Using a slotted spoon, remove the chicken from the marinade and set aside to drain slightly.

3. Place the flour, cornstarch, salt, seasoning blend, paprika, onion powder, garlic powder, and pepper in a small bowl and whisk to combine. Dredge the chicken thighs in the mixture, coating them evenly, and set aside. Place a cooling rack over a paper towel–lined baking sheet.

4. For the lemon pepper butter sauce: Place the lemon zest and juice, black pepper, salt, and melted butter in a small bowl and whisk to combine. Set aside.

5. In a 6-quart Dutch oven or heavy-bottomed pot over medium-high heat, heat 1½ inches of oil to 325°F. Gently add 2 of the chicken thighs and cook until golden brown and the internal temperature is 165°F, 6 to 7 minutes, turning over halfway through. Transfer the cooked chicken to the cooling rack and repeat with the remaining 2 chicken thighs.

6. Cut the biscuits in half and reheat if necessary (see Cook's Note). To build the sandwich, place 2 pickles on each biscuit bottom, top with the chicken thighs, and drizzle each sandwich evenly with the lemon pepper butter sauce. Cover with the biscuit tops and serve immediately.

*Cook's Note: If you are not making the sandwiches the same day, brush the cut biscuits with melted butter and reheat, cut side down, in a skillet or sauté pan over medium heat for 1 to 2 minutes.*

# Prosciutto, Cantaloupe Butter, and Afternoon Tea Biscuit Sandwich

**YIELD: 4 SERVINGS**

8 Afternoon Tea Biscuits
 (page 108)
4 tablespoons Cantaloupe
 Butter (page 151)
4 ounces thinly sliced
 prosciutto
4 ounces Green Hill cheese
 (or brie), sliced, room
 temperature
1 handful arugula
Salt and freshly ground black
 pepper, to taste

Prosciutto and melon are meant to be enjoyed together. It's a satisfying combination of salty and sweet that strikes a perfect balance. Here I've added them both, the melon in jam form, on tea biscuits spread with creamy soft cheese. Tea biscuits are smaller, appetizer-sized biscuits with a soft and airy texture from the mashed potatoes worked into the biscuit dough.

Green Hill is a soft cheese made here in Georgia by Sweet Grass Dairy. It has a silky, buttery texture that, if you're not careful, will have you consuming a whole wheel of cheese while bingeing old episodes of *227*. You can order Green Hill cheese online, or pick up some brie to use as a substitute.

Slice the biscuits in half. Spread the biscuit bottoms with cantaloupe butter. Top with a slice of prosciutto, the cheese, and some arugula. Season with salt and pepper as desired and top with the other biscuit half. Serve immediately.

# Fried Catfish and Sweet Potato Benne Seed Biscuit Sandwich

**YIELD: 4 SANDWICHES**

Four 4- to 5-ounce catfish fillets
1¼ cups full-fat buttermilk
3 tablespoons Texas Pete hot sauce
2 large eggs
½ cup self-rising flour
¼ cup cornmeal
2 tablespoons dried parsley
1½ teaspoons kosher salt
1 teaspoon smoked paprika
1 teaspoon cayenne pepper
½ teaspoon freshly ground black pepper
Peanut oil, for frying
4 Sweet Potato Benne Seed Biscuits (page 103)
¼ cup Dynamite Sauce (page 158)

Every summer when I was growing up, several fish fries would be held, from the front lawns of churches to family backyards. I'm pretty sure my granny and I attended them all. The best ones were held by the river in Cliffs of the Neuse State Park, where muddy water and thirsty mosquitos abounded. Granny would be at her most holy, singing "Down by the Riverside" as we made our way toward the sounds of grease popping and fellowship. I remember counting the bugs I'd find; I'd duck my head under the water as my granny yelled at me not to drink it. When the sun wavered and the sky started to turn different shades of orange and red, it meant it was time to get out of the water and go eat. We'd fill our plates with pieces of hot, crisp catfish that still carried oil residue, slices of white bread, and potato salad, and go sit at old wooden picnic tables that would leave splinters in your legs if you weren't careful. This was truly the best of summer.

This sandwich is in honor of those moments. The catfish is well seasoned and, paired with the punch of our Dynamite Sauce, it's perfect on a nutty, sesame-like benne seed biscuit.

1. Place the catfish fillets in a small bowl and cover with 1 cup of the buttermilk. Set aside for 15 minutes. Place a cooling rack over a paper towel–lined baking sheet.

2. Place the remaining ¼ cup buttermilk, the hot sauce, and eggs in another small bowl and whisk to combine.

3. Place the flour, cornmeal, parsley, salt, paprika, cayenne, and black pepper in a medium bowl and whisk to combine.

4. In a 6-quart Dutch oven or heavy-bottomed pot over medium-high heat, heat 1½ inches of oil to 365°F.

5. Drain the catfish. Working in batches, dip the fish fillets in the egg mixture, then in the flour mixture, and roll to coat. Carefully lower the fish, 2 pieces at a time, into the hot oil and fry until golden brown and cooked through, 5 to 6 minutes, turning over once halfway through. Be sure not to overcrowd the pan. Transfer the cooked fillets to the cooling rack to drain. Repeat with the remaining 2 fish fillets.

6. Cut the biscuits in half and reheat if necessary (see Cook's Note). To build the sandwich, place the fried catfish fillet on the bottom half of the biscuit, then drizzle with the Dynamite Sauce. Cover with the biscuit tops and serve immediately.

*Cook's Note: If you are not making the sandwiches the same day, brush the cut biscuits with melted butter and reheat, cut side down, in a skillet or sauté pan over medium heat for 1 to 2 minutes.*

*Still We Rise*

# Fried Oyster Biscuit Sandwich

YIELD: 4 SANDWICHES

12 fresh medium oysters,
   patted dry
1¼ cups full-fat buttermilk
3 tablespoons Texas Pete hot
   sauce
2 large eggs
½ cup self-rising flour
¼ cup cornmeal
2 tablespoons dried parsley
1½ teaspoons kosher salt
1 teaspoon smoked paprika
1 teaspoon cayenne pepper
½ teaspoon freshly ground
   black pepper
Peanut oil, for frying
4 Bomb Buttermilk Biscuits
   (page 33)
8 bread-and-butter pickles
¼ cup Dynamite Sauce
   (page 158)

Each year I participate in Landlocked by Oyster South, an event that benefits an organization dedicated to the advancement of aquaculture in the southern United States. It's one of the first food events that I was ever invited to participate in and felt welcomed. The first year, I made mini biscuits, and we fried oysters outside over the open flame of a Kudu grill, topping each biscuit with a remoulade-type sauce and pickles. I sort of rolled the dice on my take on an oyster po'boy in biscuit form. They were an instant hit, and we kept running out of oysters and had to shuck more.

So, each year I'm invited back, I bring the same little sliders, and each year our line gets longer, and we inevitably run out of oysters. I'm grateful for the good folks of Oyster South for the work they do and to my friends at Kimball House (Bryan, Jessie, Matt, Kizzy, and Miles) for having me each year. And if you ever ended up at the end of that line and didn't get one, I'm sorry—here's the recipe.

1. Place the oysters in a small bowl and cover with 1 cup of the buttermilk. Set aside for 15 minutes.

2. Place the remaining ¼ cup buttermilk, the hot sauce, and eggs in another small bowl and whisk to combine.

3. Place the flour, cornmeal, parsley, salt, paprika, cayenne, and black pepper in a medium bowl and whisk to combine.

4. In a 6-quart Dutch oven or heavy-bottomed pot over medium-high heat, heat 1½ inches of oil to 350°F. Place a cooling rack over a paper towel–lined baking sheet.

5. Drain the oysters. Working in batches, dip the oysters in the egg mixture, then in the flour mixture, and roll to coat. Carefully lower the oysters, 3 or 4 at a time, into the hot oil and fry until golden brown and cooked through, 3 to 4 minutes. Be sure not to overcrowd the pan. Transfer the cooked oysters to the cooling rack and drain. Repeat with the remaining oysters.

6. Cut the biscuits in half and reheat if necessary (see Cook's Note). To build the sandwich, place 2 pickles on the bottom half of each biscuit, top with 3 oysters each, and drizzle the oysters with Dynamite Sauce. Cover with the biscuit tops and serve immediately.

*Cook's Note: If you are not making the sandwiches the same day, brush the cut biscuits with melted butter and reheat, cut side down, in a skillet or sauté pan over medium heat for 1 to 2 minutes.*

# Lunch Counter Chronicles

When I was young, my mother, Renita Dortch, worked several jobs while attending graduate school. As a single parent, she was my mother, father, schoolteacher, dance recital coach—literally everything. While she didn't teach me how to bake biscuits or cakes, she taught me how to survive in a world that, as a Black woman, can sometimes seem as though it rather I not. A few times, we'd sleep on the floor in sleeping bags, telling ghost stories like we were camping: in the dark, no TV or lights. Unbeknownst to me, our thrilling camp nights were because the power had been turned off. Starting from an early age, my mother never let any obstacles get in her way. Like in 1963, when she was kicked out of the McClellan's store in our hometown for drinking from the whites-only water fountain. This unfortunate run-in at a five-and-dime store would not be her last. Years later, my mother would be one of the first Black cooks to integrate the "back" of the five-and-dime lunch counter. As it happened, it would be the very same store, McClellan's, that she was run out of as a child.

Cole slaw, onion rings, slaw dogs, even BBQ sandwiches are all on the roster of dishes my mother perfected during her tenure as a line cook at McClellan's. Once, I told her we should open a little hot dog stand to rival the local Tastee-Freez that was around the corner. Chili and melted Velveeta cheese topped with chow chow, potato chips with spicy mustard, and sweet onions and peppers were all hot dog variations of Renita's. You must split the "dog" down the middle first, then griddle it. Never boil it. Use a nice, seasoned mustard with a little bit of pickled relish if you like it basic. And smear mayo on both sides of the buns before toasting.

In April 1960, local high school students staged a protest outside the McClellan's and Woolworth's that happened to be right next to each other in our hometown of Goldsboro, North Carolina. This is the same McClellan's my mother would go on to work at.

# Pretzel Dog Biscuit

**YIELD: 4 SANDWICHES**

4 fully cooked beef bratwurst
   sausages
4 Pretzel Biscuits (page 69)
4 tablespoons Cheerwine
   Mustard (page 158)

This recipe pays homage to my mother's approach to a popular lunch counter concession, shaped by her experience working as a cook during one of this nation's most turbulent times. I like to use the pretzel biscuits, which have a unique flavor and salted tops. The sausages are split like my mother would cook her hot dogs, griddled crisp and topped with the tangy, somewhat sweet Cheerwine mustard.

1. Cut each sausage in half crosswise, then slice each half lengthwise, about two-thirds of the way through, as if you were going to stuff it. Invert and flatten into two connected halves.

2. Spray a skillet or sauté pan with nonstick cooking spray and set over medium heat. Once the pan is hot, place the sausages, sliced side down, in the pan and cook just until heated through, 3 to 4 minutes. Remove from the pan, set aside, and keep warm.

3. Cut the biscuits in half and reheat if necessary (see Cook's Note). To build the sandwich, spread 1 tablespoon of Cheerwine mustard on each bottom biscuit. Place 1 sausage on each of the bottom biscuits. Cover with the biscuit tops and serve immediately.

*Cook's Note: If you are not making the biscuits the same day, brush the cut biscuits with melted butter and reheat, cut side down, in a skillet or sauté pan over medium heat for 1 to 2 minutes.*

# The "Ultimate" Classic

YIELD: 4 SANDWICHES

4 large eggs, beaten
Salt and freshly ground black
   pepper, to taste
4 slices American or cheddar
   cheese
4 slices bacon, cooked, halved
4 Bacon Cheddar Biscuits
   (page 95)

Our second most popular sandwich at the restaurant (after our fried chicken biscuit) is an upgraded version of the classic bacon, egg, and cheese. Crispy, salty bacon is topped with buttery eggs and melting cheese, then sandwiched on a biscuit studded with bacon, cheese, black pepper, and chives. It's a sensational combination of all my favorite ingredients in each bite.

1. Spray a cast-iron pan (either a frying pan or griddle) with nonstick cooking spray and heat over medium. Add the eggs and cook until almost set, seasoning with salt and pepper as desired. Divide the eggs into 4 equal parts in the pan and top each portion with a slice of cheese and continue to cook until the eggs are set and the cheese has melted slightly.

2. Cut the biscuits in half and reheat if necessary (see Cook's Note).

3. To build the sandwich, layer the biscuit bottom with bacon, then using a spatula, transfer the eggs with melted cheese on top of the bacon. Top with the biscuit top. Serve immediately or wrap for an on-the-go breakfast!

*Cook's Note: If you are not making the sandwiches the same day, brush the cut biscuits with melted butter and reheat, cut side down, in a skillet or sauté pan over medium heat for 1 to 2 minutes.*

# Lox and Loaded Biscuit Sandwich

**YIELD: 4 SANDWICHES**

6 ounces cream cheese, room
   temperature
2 tablespoons freshly squeezed
   lemon juice
4 teaspoons capers, drained
1 tablespoon chopped fresh dill
   (optional)
Salt and freshly ground black
   pepper, to taste
4 Everything "Bagel" Biscuits
   (page 92)
6 ounces smoked salmon,
   thinly sliced
⅓ cup sliced red onion

This biscuit sandwich is a riff on the much-loved bagel that's loaded with cream cheese, red onion, and smoked salmon. You get a nice smokiness from the salmon and a tang from the cream cheese. Capers, dill, and red onion add some zing. A wonderful balance of flavors and textures.

1.  Combine the cream cheese, lemon juice, capers, dill (if using), and salt and pepper in a small bowl.

2.  Cut the biscuits in half and reheat if necessary (see Cook's Note). To build the sandwich, spread the cream cheese mixture on each half of the biscuit. Top with the smoked salmon and red onions.

*Cook's Note: If you are not making the sandwiches the same day, brush the cut biscuits with melted butter and reheat, cut side down, in a skillet or sauté pan over medium heat for 1 to 2 minutes.*

# Sweet Potato Bis-cakes

YIELD: 8 TO 10 PANCAKES

¾ cup / 113 grams all-purpose
  flour
3 tablespoons sugar
2 teaspoons baking powder
½ teaspoon kosher salt
¼ teaspoon ground cinnamon
¼ teaspoon ground nutmeg
½ cup cooked mashed sweet
  potatoes, room temperature
1 large egg, room temperature
1 cup whole milk, room
  temperature
2 tablespoons unsalted butter,
  melted and cooled slightly,
  plus more for the griddle

I wish I could offer some compelling story about these "bis-cakes." The truth is, I once tried to make biscuits and added way too much milk. As I went to throw out the mess I'd made, my granny stopped me and asked if I'd lost my mind for throwing out food. Her suggestion? Put a skillet on the stove and cook them like pancakes. Well, of course!

So, this recipe is a result of my failure years ago, which I've adapted into my go-to pancake recipe. Since this is a cookbook and I'm trying to be a little bit bougie, I've incorporated the golden vegetable of North Carolina: sweet potatoes. Spiked with cinnamon and nutmeg, these pancakes have a delicate texture and a flavor that is more savory than sweet. The next time you make sweet potatoes, mash and save a half cup for these bis-cakes!

1. Place the flour, sugar, baking powder, salt, cinnamon, and nutmeg in a medium bowl and whisk to combine.

2. Place the mashed sweet potatoes, egg, milk, and butter in a small bowl and whisk to combine.

3. Add the sweet potato mixture to the flour mixture and stir with a spatula until a batter forms. Set aside for 5 minutes.

4. Heat a griddle over medium heat and lightly grease it with a pat of butter. Using a ¼-cup measure, scoop the batter onto the hot griddle and cook until bubbles form around the edges and the pancake is golden brown, about 2 minutes. Flip and continue cooking until cooked through, 2 to 3 more minutes. Serve immediately or stack in a warm oven until ready to serve. Repeat with the remaining batter. Serve with smears of apple butter between each pancake or warm maple syrup.

# Biscuit-Crusted Breakfast Quiche

YIELD: 8 TO 10 SERVINGS

## BISCUIT CRUST

2 cups / 240 grams all-purpose
  flour, plus extra for rolling
  and shaping
1 tablespoon baking powder
1 teaspoon kosher salt
6 tablespoons unsalted butter,
  cold, cut into ½-inch pieces
1 cup full-fat buttermilk, cold

## FILLING

4 large eggs
½ cup whole milk
½ cup heavy cream
½ teaspoon kosher salt
¼ teaspoon freshly ground
  black pepper
½ cup (4 ounces) shredded
  cheddar cheese
2 cups (8 ounces) cooked
  ground breakfast sausage,
  drained

Growing up, we didn't go out to eat often, and we hardly ever went "out" for breakfast. Mother's Day was an exception. We would have brunch at a chain hotel in our city (the Radisson, I believe, but don't quote me on that). The buffet always had a vast array of items served in silver chafing dishes, from French toast—my personal favorite—to pineapple-glazed ham that was labeled "Canadian bacon." (This was North Carolina, so we called it ham.)

We ate on white china and drank tea out of enameled teacups. My granny, Geraldine, would critique every bit of food she piled up on her plate. There were always these little egg pies with bits of bacon and cheese encased in a flaky pastry crust. You could peel them out of the little paper shells they were baked in and eat them whole. Absolutely outstanding. Granny would tell me not to eat too many. She would say, "I believe these are those eggs that come in a carton; those aren't eggs from chickens."

Well, I never forgot those little egg pies, and once a month at the restaurant, we run a special of quiche in a biscuit crust. This recipe calls for 4 large eggs, from chickens. The combination of milk and heavy cream gives this quiche the richest filling, and you can customize it with your own additions such as bacon, caramelized onions, or spinach. Using a food processor works best, but this recipe can be made without one.

1. For the biscuit crust: In the bowl of a food processor, place the flour, baking powder, and salt and pulse 3 to 4 times to combine. Scatter the butter on the flour mixture and pulse until the mixture resembles a coarse crumble, 4 to 5 pulses. Add the buttermilk and pulse until a dough forms and pulls away from the sides of the food processor bowl, 4 to 5 more pulses.

2. Remove the dough from the food processor and divide in half, forming 2 disks. Wrap each half with plastic wrap and refrigerate a minimum of 2 hours or up to overnight. You will need only 1 disk for this recipe. The other can be stored, well-wrapped, in the freezer for up to 2 months.

*Recipe continues*

3. On a floured work surface, roll out 1 of the disks of chilled dough. Turn the dough a quarter turn after every few rolls until you have a 12-inch circle. Carefully place the dough into a 9-inch pie dish. Tuck it in with your fingers, making sure it is completely smooth. To make a lovely edge, do not trim the excess dough. Instead, fold the excess back over the edge and use your hands to mold the edge into a rim around the pie. Crimp the edges with a fork or use your fingers to flute the edges. Refrigerate until ready to use.

4. For the filling and baking: Adjust the oven rack to the middle position and preheat the oven to 375°F.

5. Place the eggs in a large bowl and whisk until light yellow in color. Add the milk, heavy cream, salt, and pepper and whisk until combined.

6. Spread the sausage onto the prepared crust and sprinkle the cheddar on top. Then pour the egg mixture over the bacon and cheddar. Bake 50 to 60 minutes, until the quiche is just set, only slightly jiggly in the middle, and slightly golden brown. Cool 10 to 15 minutes before slicing and serving.

# Biscuit Bread Pudding with Whiskey Cream Sauce

YIELD: 8 TO 10 SERVINGS

## BREAD PUDDING

8 cups (12 ounces) cubed leftover biscuits (6 to 7 biscuits)

2 tablespoons salted butter, melted and cooled slightly

¾ cup whole milk

½ cup heavy cream

2 large eggs, beaten

½ cup sugar

½ teaspoon ground cinnamon

½ teaspoon vanilla extract

¼ teaspoon ground nutmeg

## WHISKEY CREAM SAUCE

1 cup heavy cream

2 tablespoons sugar

2 tablespoons unsalted butter

1 tablespoon bourbon

In *The Up South Cookbook*, my dear friend Nicole Taylor instructs us not to throw away day-old biscuits. Instead, she advises toasting them and using them as bread crumbs. I can attest both that this is a great idea and that Nicole always gives the best advice.

That said, the idea of leftover biscuits seems insane to me. Who doesn't eat them all? Well, it happens, and as Nicole says, you should never waste a good biscuit. Another delicious way to repurpose leftover biscuits, or any kind of bread for that matter, is to turn them into bread pudding. I love bread pudding with just powdered sugar sprinkled over the top, but a good cream sauce gives it a bit more sophistication and adds a depth of flavor, especially when you pour in a little bourbon. My aunt Rene used to go around the neighborhood collecting the "heels" of bread loaves. She'd take those pieces and make unbelievable bread pudding that was served at the community center or church at the end of the week.

Bread pudding is one of the most delicious ways to prevent food waste. Using leftover biscuits to bake into a custard produces bread pudding that, when sliced, tastes like French toast. Something about the egg- and milk-based custard baking into a buttery biscuit brings out an absolute melt-in-your-mouth dessert with crispy tops that still taste like a buttermilk biscuit.

1. For the bread pudding: Preheat the oven to 350°F. Spray an 8 × 8-inch baking dish with nonstick cooking spray.

2. Place the biscuit cubes in a medium bowl and set aside. Place the butter, milk, cream, eggs, sugar, cinnamon, vanilla, and nutmeg in a separate medium bowl and whisk to combine.

3. Pour the milk mixture over the biscuit cubes and stir until well combined. Set aside for 30 minutes so the biscuits can absorb some of the liquid.

4. Pour the mixture into the prepared baking dish and bake for 30 to 35 minutes, until golden brown and a toothpick inserted in the center comes out clean. Set aside to cool slightly.

5. For the sauce: In a small saucepan over medium heat, combine the heavy cream, sugar, and butter and cook, stirring occasionally, until the butter is melted and the sauce has thickened and reduced slightly, about 10 minutes. Add the bourbon and cook, stirring continuously, until the sauce coats the back of a spoon.

6. Pour the sauce over the warm bread pudding and serve immediately. Refrigerate any unused portions for up to 3 days.

## RESOURCES

**Mildred "Mama" Dip Council,** *Mama Dip's Kitchen*

**Cleora Butler,** *Cleora's Kitchen*

**Princess Pamela,** *The Soul Food Cookbook*

**Sallie Ann Robinson,** *Gullah Home Cooking the Daufuskie Way*

**Lena Richards,** *New Orleans Cookbook*

**Norma Jean & Carole Darden,** *Spoonbread & Strawberry Wine*

**Freda DeKnight,** *A Date with a Dish*

**Joyce White,** *Soul Food: Recipes and Reflections from the African-American Church*

**Leah Chase,** *The Dooky Chase Cookbook*

**Nicole Taylor,** *The Up South Cookbook*

**Sheila Ferguson,** *Soul Food: Classic Cuisine from the Deep South*

**Psyche Williams-Forson,** *Building Houses out of Chicken Legs*

**Edna Lewis,** *In Pursuit of Flavor*

# Acknowledgments

*In writing this book, I've learned the importance of giving people their "flowers" while they are still here to know what they mean to you.*

**To my family:** First and foremost, I'd like to thank my husband and business partner, Charles Reeves, who's spent countless hours and resources to make my dreams become a reality when you'd much rather be at home watching the Eagles play. None of this would be possible without your love and support. Words could never express how much that means to me.

My daughter, Kamaya Council, who at times doubled as my assistant baker, web/social media guru, and everything else when I needed the help. All while navigating college course work. My angel girl.

My son, Charlie Reeves, a lover of good biscuits, apple butter, and his mama. Thanks for the encouraging hugs every day.

Charles Reeves Sr., Marian, Debbie, and Maya Joy Reeves, thank you for sharing your stories for this book and all the love and encouragement.

My dear Mama, Renita Bates, thank you for a lifetime of love and strength.

**To my team:** This book would not be possible without hours of recipe testing and re-testing and more testing. I'm forever grateful for Chef Mary Schowe, a.k.a. my right and left hands in the kitchen. And thank you Jayla Smith, Tamie Cook, Mike Sheats, and Benita Fowler.

**To my literary agents:** Thank you Sally Ekus and Lisa Ekus for believing in me very early on and for all your literary savvy along the way.

**To my Bomb Biscuit Co. staff/family:** You keep the biscuit love churning, and I love y'all. Thank you for putting up with me writing a book in the middle of opening and expanding a restaurant, because who in their right mind would ever do that?

My daughter Kamaya and me.

To photographer Andrew Thomas Lee and food stylist Thom Driver: Thank you for bringing this book to life with your beautiful images and artistic direction. The talent you possess is unmatched! I love y'all forever!

To the wonderful team at Clarkston Potter: Thank you for your guidance on this book journey. Francis Lam, thank you for believing in the idea of this book and for your support. Susan Roxborough, you're one of the kindest and most patient people I've ever met; I owe you a lifetime of biscuits. Ian Dingman, Darian Keels, Serena Wang, Jessica Heim, and all those who have helped along the way, thank you isn't enough, but one day I'm going to bring y'all a basket full of fried chicken biscuits because I was taught the best way to show thanks is through fried chicken.

To the "Saints" of St. James AME Zion Church of Goldsboro, North Carolina, who ran the church kitchen: You all shaped my life, and I'm here today because of the nourishment, both body and soul, shown to me in the halls of this church.

To a host of good folks who have in big and small ways encouraged and supported me, the restaurant, and this book: My guardian angel Valerie Boyd, Roz Bentley, Bryan Furman, Bryant Terry, Jessica B. Harris, Toni Tipton-Martin, Nicole Taylor, Michael Twitty, Julia Turshen, Adrian Miller, Bill Smith, John T. Edge, Afton Thomas, the Southern Foodways Alliance, Thérèse Nelson, Nancie McDermott, Todd Richards, Greg Collier, Keia Mastrianni, Mashama Bailey, Valerie Irwin, Jocelyn Delk Adams, Cheryl Day, Cynthia Graubart, Virginia Willis, Tiffanie Barriere, Kristie Abney, Megan Dekok, Cindy Rahe, Nik Sharma, Matt and Ted Lee, and so, so many more.

To every customer who graces our little biscuit establishment, thank you for the love and support!

# Index

Pages with photos are in *italic*.

Published in the United States by Clarkson Potter/Publishers, an imprint of Random House, a division of Penguin Random House LLC, New York.
ClarksonPotter.com | RandomHouseBooks.com

CLARKSON POTTER is a trademark and POTTER with colophon is a registered trademark of Penguin Random House LLC.

Library of Congress Cataloging-in-Publication Data
Names: Council, Erika, author.
Title: Still we rise / Erika Council.
Description: New York : Clarkson Potter, [2023]. | Includes index. |
Identifiers: LCCN 2022045287 (print) | LCCN 2022045288 (ebook) | ISBN 9780593236093 (hardcover) | ISBN 9780593236109 (ebook)
Subjects: LCSH: Biscuits. | Cooking, American--Southern style. | LCGFT: Cookbooks.
Classification: LCC TX770.B55 C68 2023 (print) | LCC TX770.B55 (ebook) | DDC 641.81/5--dc23/eng/20220926
LC record available at https://lccn.loc.gov/2022045287
LC ebook record available at https://lccn.loc.gov/2022045288

ISBN 978-0-593-23609-3
eISBN 978-0-593-23610-9

Printed in China

Photographer: Andrew Lee
Food Stylist: Thom Driver
Editors: Francis Lam and Susan Roxborough
Editorial Assistant: Darian Keels
Designer: Ian Dingman
Production Editor: Serena Wang
Production Manager: Jessica Heim
Compositors: Merri Ann Morrell and Hannah Hunt
Copy Editor: Heather Rodino
Indexer: Jay Kreider
Marketer: Joseph Lozada
Publicist: Kristin Casemore
Cover photographs by: Andrew Lee

10 9 8 7 6 5 4 3 2 1

First Edition